Consciousness
The Missing Link

Scientists of the Bhaktivedanta Institute examine key underlying concepts of the modern life sciences in light of India's age-old Vedic knowledge. With an introductory survey of the issues by the Institute's founder, His Divine Grace A. C. Bhaktivedanta Swami Prabhupāda.

THE BHAKTIVEDANTA BOOK TRUST

Los Angeles · New York · London · Paris · Zürich · Bombay

Readers interested in the subject matter of this book
are invited by the International Society for Krishna Consciousness
to visit any ISKCON center worldwide (see address list in back
of book) or to correspond with the Secretary:

International Society for Krishna Consciousness
3764 Watseka Avenue
Los Angeles, California 90034

First Printing, 1980: 230,000 copies

Reprints of Prior Publications
© 1979, 1980 Bhaktivedanta Book Trust
All Rights Reserved
Printed in the United States of America

Library of Congress Catalog Card Number: 80-54641
International Standard Book Number: 0-89213-108-X

Contents

Introduction   *v*

I. The Goal of Knowledge   **1**
   a conversation with His Divine Grace
   A. C. Bhaktivedanta Swami Prabhupāda

II. On Inspiration   **23**
    by Sadāpūta dāsa

III. The Computerized Mr. Jones   **37**
     by Sadāpūta dāsa

IV. The Principle of Reincarnation   **57**
    by Bhaktisvarūpa Dāmodara Swami

About the Authors   **69**

BOOKS by
His Divine Grace
A. C. Bhaktivedanta Swami Prabhupāda

Bhagavad-gītā As It Is
Śrīmad-Bhāgavatam, cantos 1–10 (30 vols.)
Śrī Caitanya-caritāmṛta (17 vols.)
Teachings of Lord Caitanya
The Nectar of Devotion
The Nectar of Instruction
Śrī Īśopaniṣad
Easy Journey to Other Planets
Kṛṣṇa Consciousness: The Topmost Yoga System
Kṛṣṇa, the Supreme Personality of Godhead (3 vols.)
Perfect Questions, Perfect Answers
Dialectical Spiritualism—A Vedic View of Western Philosophy
Teachings of Lord Kapila, the Son of Devahūti
Transcendental Teachings of Prahlād Mahārāja
Teachings of Queen Kuntī
Kṛṣṇa, the Reservoir of Pleasure
The Science of Self-Realization
The Path of Perfection
Life Comes From Life
The Perfection of Yoga
Beyond Birth and Death
On the Way to Kṛṣṇa
Geetār-gan (Bengali)
Vairāgya-vidyā (Bengali)
Buddhi-yoga (Bengali)
Bhakti-ratna-bolī (Bengali)
Rāja-vidyā: The King of Knowledge
Elevation to Kṛṣṇa Consciousness
Kṛṣṇa Consciousness: The Matchless Gift
Back to Godhead magazine (founder)

A complete catalog is available upon request.

Bhaktivedanta Book Trust
3764 Watseka Avenue
Los Angeles, California 90034

Introduction

In cultures throughout the world, people have traditionally believed that the innermost self of each human being is an entity that is distinct from the gross physical body. Many religious authorities have maintained that this self, or soul, possesses properties that are quite different from those of matter, and that it survives the death of the physical body. In recent years, however, with the development of modern empirical science, great skepticism has arisen in the minds of many educated people about the existence of the self as a distinct entity.

Investigators in different scientific fields such as chemistry, biology, and psychology have found no clear evidence for the existence of a nonphysical conscious entity, although they have been able to make many advances in their efforts to explain the physical phenomena of the body in mechanistic terms. Philosophers, far from demonstrating the existence of such an entity, have been unable to reach any clear consensus on what its properties may be, and the adherents of many different religious sects have been unable to agree on a consistent description of the nonphysical self that is capable of practical verification. As a result, many scientists have completely rejected the idea of a nonphysical self and have adopted the view that the self is nothing more than an interplay of phenomena within the brain that completely obey known physical laws. Owing to the prestige of modern science, this view has been widely accepted by educated people throughout the world.

The thesis of this book is that scientists have adopted these conclusions prematurely. It is indeed true that modern Western science, in its present state of development, has been unable to shed any light on the possible characteristics of the transcendental self. Nonetheless, a genuine science of the nonphysical self is not only possible but already exists, and it has been known since time immemorial. This is the science of self-realization expounded in the Vedic literatures of India, such as *Bhagavad-gītā* and *Śrīmad-Bhāgavatam.*

Like any genuine science, the science of self-realization consists of both theoretical principles and practical methods whereby these principles can be verified by direct experience. The exponents of Vedic science agree with modern scientific researchers in viewing the body as an elaborate machine. However, they go beyond the limited mechanistic viewpoint and present a detailed description of the conscious self and its relation with the material body that is unrivaled for its clarity and logical coherence. Even though it entails many concepts that lie beyond the scope of current scientific investigations, this description is not simply an arbitrary body of dogma, for it is accompanied by exacting procedures of verification and is of great practical value. As such, the Vedic science of self-realization invites modern scientists to modify and enlarge their scientific world view.

In the first part of this book the basic principles of this science are discussed in a conversation between His Divine Grace A. C. Bhaktivedanta Swami Prabhupāda, the world's foremost authority on Vedic philosophy, and Dr. Gregory Benford, a professor of physics from the University of California. Śrīla Prabhupāda points out that Vedic principles, when properly understood, do not conflict with the factual findings of modern Western science. He observes, however, that the predominant perspective of modern science is too narrow, and that scientists err when they jump to the conclusion that their present picture of reality is complete in its essential features. He suggests that scientists can extend and perfect their understanding by systematically taking into account the higher principles of the Vedic science of self-realization.

The remainder of this book presents three essays showing that this suggestion can be practically carried out. These essays were written by two professional scientists, Dr. T. D. Singh (Bhaktisvarūpa Dāmodara Swami) and Sadāpūta dāsa, who are both disciples of Śrīla Prabhupāda. In the first two essays, Sadāpūta dāsa discusses some of the modern scientific theories about the nature of the conscious mind and shows how these theories can be improved and extended when considered in the light of Vedic scientific knowledge. In the third essay, Dr. Singh discusses the Vedic concept of the nonphysical self in detail and shows how the science of self-realization is of great practical value in everyday life.

Says biophysicist D. P. Dubey of Harvard Medical School, "We may lead ourselves down a blind alley by adhering dogmatically to the assumption that life can be explained entirely by what we now know of the laws of nature. . . . By remaining open to the ideas embodied in the Vedic tradition of India, modern scientists can see their own disciplines from a new perspective and further the real aim of all scientific endeavor: the search for truth."

—The Publishers

CHAPTER I

THE GOAL OF KNOWLEDGE

A Conversation with
His Divine Grace A. C. Bhaktivedanta
Swami Prabhupāda

In the following conversation His Divine Grace A.C. Bhaktivedanta Swami Prabhupāda, founder-*ācārya* of the International Society for Krishna Consciousness (ISKCON), and Dr. Gregory Benford, a professor of physics at the University of California, Irvine, discuss the Vedic concepts of the self and consciousness as they relate to the views of modern science.

Śrīla Prabhupāda: By "scientific advancement" do you mean the advancement from bullock cart to motorcar? If we can advance from the stage of the bullock cart to the stage of the fine mechanical arrangement of the motorcar, you take it to be advancement of science, do you not?

Dr. Benford: It is advancement of technology.

Śrīla Prabhupāda: Technology or science, it is the same thing. Our problem is the advancement of the spirit soul. So what is the scientific knowledge about the spirit soul?

Dr. Benford: There is virtually no scientific knowledge about the spirit soul.

Śrīla Prabhupāda: Therefore there is actually no advancement of scientific knowledge.

Dr. Benford: Well, scientific knowledge is a different class of knowledge. Out of many different classes of knowledge, you may feel that one type of knowledge is better than another, but that is a different question.

Śrīla Prabhupāda: Perhaps. There are different departments of knowledge. For example, in medical science there is one department to study the physiology and anatomy of the body. That is one department of knowledge. But beyond this body there is mind and intelligence. That is studied by psychology. That is also science, mental science.

Dr. Benford: It is science at a very crude stage of development.

Śrīla Prabhupāda: That may be, but it is still accepted as science, is it not? Psychology and metaphysics deal with the mind and intelligence. And beyond that there is the spirit soul. There are so many departments of knowledge: the medical study of the body, the psychological study of the mind, and ultimately there is spiritual, transcendental knowledge. The body and mind are simply the coverings of the spirit soul, just as your body is covered by this shirt and coat. If you simply take care of the shirt and coat and neglect the person who is covered by this shirt and coat, do you think that this is advancement of knowledge?

Dr. Benford: I think that there is no category of knowledge that is useless.

Śrīla Prabhupāda: We don't say that this scientific knowledge is useless. Mechanics, electronics—this is also knowledge. But different departments of knowledge differ in their comparative importance. For example, if someone wants to cook nicely, this is also a science. There are many different departments of knowledge, but the central point is the knowledge of the soul, *ātma-jñāna*.

Dr. Benford: I feel that you have advanced a position I cannot agree with entirely, but I think it is certainly logical. The only form of knowledge that is verifiable—that is, verifiable in the sense of getting everybody to agree with it—is that which can be proved logically or experimentally.

Śrīla Prabhupāda: The science of the spirit soul can be verified logically.

Dr. Benford: How so?

Śrīla Prabhupāda: Just consider your body. You once had the body of a child, but now you don't have that body anymore; you have a different body. Yet, anyone can understand that you once had the body of a child. This is a fact. So your body has changed, but you are still remaining.

Dr. Benford: I am not so sure it is the same "I."

Śrīla Prabhupāda: Yes, you are the same "I." Just as the parents of a child will say, after he has grown up, "Oh, just see how our son has grown." He is the same person: his parents say so, his friends say so, his family says so—everyone says so. This is the evidence. You have to accept this point, because there is so much evidence. Even your mother will deny that you are a different person, even though you have a different body.

Dr. Benford: But I may not be the same being that I was.

Śrīla Prabhupāda: Correct. "Not the same" means, for example, that a young child may talk nonsense now, but when he is grown up and gets an adult body he does not speak foolishly. Although he is the same person, along with his change in body he has developed different consciousness. But the spirit soul, the person, is the same. He acts according to his body, that's all—according to his circumstances. A dog, for example, is also a spirit soul, but because he has a dog's body he lives and acts like a dog. Similarly, the spirit soul, when he has a child's body, acts like a child. When he has a different body, the same soul acts like a man. According to circumstances, his activities are changing, but the person is the same. For example, you are a scientist. In your childhood you were not a scientist, so your dealings at that time were not those of a scientist. One's dealings may change according to circumstances, but the person is the same.

Therefore, the conclusion is, as stated in the *Bhagavad-gītā* [2.13], *tathā dehāntara-prāptir dhīras tatra na muhyati:* "When this body is finished, the soul gives it up and accepts another body." *Tathā dehāntara. Dehāntara* means "another body." This is our Sanskrit knowledge from the *Bhagavad-gītā.* When the spirit soul is injected into the womb of a woman, it forms a little body. Gradually, through the emulsification of secretions, the body develops to the size of a pea, because of the presence of the spirit soul. Gradually the body develops nine holes—eyes, ears, mouth, nostrils, genital, and rectum. In this way the body is developed to completion in seven months. Then consciousness comes.

Dr. Benford: At seven months?

Śrīla Prabhupāda: Yes. The child wants to come out. He feels uncomfortable, therefore he prays to God to kindly release him from this bondage. He promises to become a devotee of God when he gets out. So he comes out of the womb after ten months. But unless his parents are devotees, due to circumstances he forgets God. Only if the father and mother are devotees does he continue his God consciousness. Therefore, it is a great good fortune to take birth in a family of Vaiṣṇavas, those who are God conscious. This God consciousness is real scientific knowledge.

Dr. Benford: Is it true that the children of all such parents are somewhat spiritually superior to the children of other parents?

Śrīla Prabhupāda: Generally, yes. They get the opportunity of being trained by the mother and father. Fortunately, my father was a great devotee, so I received this training from the very beginning. Somehow or other we had this spark of Kṛṣṇa consciousness, and our father detected it. Then I accepted my spiritual master. In this way I have come to this stage of *sannyāsa*. I am very much indebted to my father, for he took care of me in such a way that I became perfectly Kṛṣṇa conscious. My father used to receive many saintly persons at our home, and to every one of them he used to say, "Kindly bless my son so that he may become a servant of Rādhārāṇī." That was his only ambition. He taught me how to play the *mṛdaṅga*, but my mother was not very satisfied. She would say, "Why are you teaching him to play *mṛdaṅga*?" But my father would say, "No, no, he must learn a little *mṛdaṅga*." My father was very affectionate to me. He never chastised me. Therefore, if by his past pious activities one gets a good father and mother, that is a great chance for advancing in Kṛṣṇa consciousness.

Dr. Benford: What will happen to you next?

Śrīla Prabhupāda: We are going back to Kṛṣṇa. We have got everything: Kṛṣṇa's name, Kṛṣṇa's address, Kṛṣṇa's form, Kṛṣṇa's activities. We know everything, and we are going there. Kṛṣṇa has assured us of this in the *Bhagavad-gītā* [4.9], *tyaktvā dehaṁ punar janma naiti mām eti so 'rjuna:* "Upon leaving the body, he does not take his birth again in this material world, but attains My eternal abode, O Arjuna." And not only the devotee attains this, but anyone who understands Kṛṣṇa. This is stated in the *Bhagavad-gītā* [4.9], *janma karma ca me divyam evaṁ yo vetti tattvataḥ:* "One who knows Me in truth, scientifically," Kṛṣṇa says, "is eligible to enter into the kingdom of God."

Dr. Benford: How do you know that people return in some other form?

Śrīla Prabhupāda: We see that there are so many forms. Where do these different forms come from? The form of the dog, the form of the cat, the form of the tree, the form of the reptile, the forms of the insects, the forms of the fish? What is your explanation for all these different forms? That you do not know.

Dr. Benford: Evolution.

Śrīla Prabhupāda: There may be evolution, but at the same time all the different species are existing. The fish is existing, man is existing, the tiger is existing, everyone is existing. It is just like the different types of apartments here in Los Angeles. You may occupy one of them, according to your ability to pay rent, but all types of apartments are nevertheless existing at the same time. Similarly, the living entity, according to his *karma,* is given facility to occupy one of these bodily forms. But there is evolution also. From the fish, the next stage of evolution is to plant life. From plant forms the living entity may enter an insect body. From the insect body the next stage is bird, then beast, and finally the spirit soul may evolve to the human form of life. And from the human form, if one becomes qualified, he may evolve further. Otherwise, he must again enter the evolutionary cycle. Therefore, this human form of life is an important junction in the evolutionary development of the living entity.

As stated in the *Bhagavad-gītā* [9.25]:

> *yānti deva-vratā devān*
> *pitṝn yānti pitṛ-vratāḥ*
> *bhūtāni yānti bhūtejyā*
> *yānti mad-yājino pi mām*

"Those who worship the demigods will take birth among the demigods; those who worship ghosts and spirits will take birth among such beings; those who worship ancestors go to the ancestors; and those who worship Me will live with Me." There are different *lokas,* or planetary systems, and you can go to the higher planetary systems where the demigods live and take a body there, or you can go where the Pitās, or ancestors, live. You can take a body here in Bhūloka, the earthly planetary system, or you can go to the planet of God, Kṛṣṇaloka. Whatever you like, you can achieve. This method of transferring oneself at the time of death to whatever planet one chooses is called *yoga*. There is a physical process of *yoga*, a philosophical process of *yoga*, and a devotional process of *yoga*. The devotees can go directly to the planet where Kṛṣṇa is.

Dr. Benford: Undoubtedly you are aware that there are a few people, both in Eastern and Western society, who feel that it is a bit more intellectually justifiable to be completely agnostic about matters of theology. They feel, more or less, that if God had wanted us to know something more about Him, then He would have made it more easily apprehendable.

Śrīla Prabhupāda: Then you don't believe in God?

Dr. Benford: I don't *not* believe in God; I'm just not forming an opinion until I have some evidence.

Śrīla Prabhupāda: But do you think that there is a God or not?

Dr. Benford: I have a suspicion that there may be, but it is unverified.

Śrīla Prabhupāda: Suspicion, doubt. That means you are not quite confident.

Dr. Benford: Yes.

Śrīla Prabhupāda: But you think sometimes that there may be God, do you not?

Dr. Benford: Yes.

Śrīla Prabhupāda: So you are in doubt, suspicion—you are not certain—but your inclination is that you think there is God, is it not? Your knowledge being imperfect, you are in doubt, that's all. Otherwise you are inclined to think of God. That is your position. But because you are a scientific man, unless you perceive it scientifically you do not accept. That is your position. But from your side, you believe in God.

Dr. Benford: Sometimes.

Śrīla Prabhupāda: Yes. Sometimes, or all times, it doesn't matter. That is the position of everyone. As long as one is in the human form of life, whether he is civilized or uncivilized doesn't matter: everyone has dormant consciousness of God. It simply has to be developed by proper training. It is just like anything else in life. For example, you have become a scientist by proper training, proper education. Similarly, the dormant consciousness of God, or Kṛṣṇa, is there in everyone. It simply requires proper education to awaken it. However, this education is not given in the universities. That is the defect in modern education. Although the inclination to be Kṛṣṇa conscious is there, the authorities are unfortunately not giving any education about God. Therefore people are becoming godless, and they are feeling baffled in obtaining the true joy and satisfaction of life.

In San Diego, some priestly orders are going to hold a meeting to investigate the reasons why people are becoming averse to religion and not coming to church. But the cause is simple. Because our government does not know that life, especially human life, is meant for understanding God, they are supporting all the departments of knowledge very nicely except the principal department, God consciousness.

Dr. Benford: So of course, the reason is that—

Śrīla Prabhupāda: Reasons there may be many, but the principal reason is that this age is the Kali-yuga. People are not very intelligent, therefore they are trying to avoid this department of knowledge, the most important department of knowledge. And they are simply busy in the departments of knowledge in which the animals are also busy. Your advancement of knowledge is comprised of four things—eating, sleeping, mating, and defending. For example, you are discovering so many lethal weapons, and the politicians are taking advantage of it for defending. You are discovering so many chemicals to check pregnancy, and they are using them to increase sex life.

Dr. Benford: What is going to the moon?

Śrīla Prabhupāda: That is also sleeping. You go there and sleep and spend money, that's all. Otherwise, what can you do there?

Dr. Benford: You can go there and learn.

Śrīla Prabhupāda: You go there and sleep, that's all. Sleeping. You are spending billions and getting nothing in return.

Dr. Benford: It seems worth more than that.

Śrīla Prabhupāda: No, nothing more, because these four principles—eating, sleeping, mating, and defending—are the background. If you have no knowledge beyond this body, you cannot go beyond this bodily category. You have no other jurisdiction of knowledge. It may be very gorgeous, polished bodily knowledge, but your whole range of activities is within these four principles of eating, sleeping, mating, and defending. This knowledge is prevalent among the lower animals also. They know how to eat, they know how to sleep, they know how to have sexual intercourse, and they also know how to defend.

Dr. Benford: But they don't know anything about nuclear physics!

Śrīla Prabhupāda: That does not mean that you are improved over the animals. It is the same thing, only polished, that's all. You are improving from the bullock cart to the motorcar, that's all. It is simply a transformation of material knowledge.

Dr. Benford: There is knowledge about the structure of the physical world.

Śrīla Prabhupāda: But it is a waste of energy, because in your activities you cannot go beyond this bodily jurisdiction of eating, sleeping, mating, and defending. You may make a very nice apartment for sleeping, but when you sleep you get the same quality of enjoyment as when the dog sleeps. The dog may sleep on the ground, and you may sleep in a very nice apartment, but when you are asleep your condition and the condition of the dog are the same. You may be sleeping in a nice apartment and he may sleep on the grass, but both of you are forgetting everything. You forget that you are sleeping in a nice estate or in a nice skyscraper building, and the dog forgets that he is sleeping on the ground. But what is the use of this nice apartment? When you sleep there, the dog and you become one. You may have so many electrical appliances and other material conveniences, but when you sleep you forget everything. Therefore this gorgeous sleeping accommodation is simply a waste of time.

Dr. Benford: You seem to place emphasis on what knowledge does for you. What about the sheer joy of discovering how nature works? For example, now we think that we understand matter like this [*he indicates the grass on which they are sitting*]. We think that we know from experiments, theory, and analysis that it is made up of particles that we cannot see, and we can analyze the properties of it through experiment. We know that it is made up of molecules. We understand some of the forces that hold it together, and this is the first time we knew this. We didn't know it before.

Śrīla Prabhupāda: But what is the benefit? Although you know every particle of this grass, what benefit is derived out of it? The grass is growing. It will grow with or without your knowledge. You may know it or not know it, but it will not make any difference. Anything you like you may study from a material, analytical point of view. Any nonsense thing you take you can study and study and compile a voluminous book. But what will be the use of it?

Dr. Benford: I seem to view the world as—

Śrīla Prabhupāda: Suppose I take this grass. I can write volumes of books—when it came into existence, when it died, what are the fibers, what are the molecules. In so many ways I can describe this insignificant foliage. But what is the use of it?

Dr. Benford: If it has no use, why did God put it there? Isn't it worthwhile studying?

Śrīla Prabhupāda: Our point is that you would rather study the insignificant grass than the God who has created everything. If you could understand Him, automatically you would study the grass. But you want to separate His grass from Him, to study it separately. In this way you can compile volumes and volumes on the subject, but why waste your intelligence in that way? The branch of a tree is beautiful as long as it is attached to the main trunk, but as soon as you cut it off it will dry up. Therefore, what is the use of studying the dried-up branch? It is a waste of intelligence.

Dr. Benford: But why is it a waste?

Śrīla Prabhupāda: Certainly it is a waste, because the result is not useful.

Dr. Benford: Well, what is useful?

Śrīla Prabhupāda: It is useful to know yourself, what you are.

Dr. Benford: Why is knowledge of myself better than knowledge of a plant?

Śrīla Prabhupāda: If you understand what you are, then you understand other things. That is called *ātma-tattva, ātma-jñāna,* self-knowledge. *That* is important. I am a spirit soul, and I am passing through so many species of life. But what is my position? I don't wish to die, because I am afraid to change bodies. Therefore, I am afraid of death. This question should be raised first: I don't want unhappiness, but unhappiness comes. I don't want death, but death comes. I don't want disease, but disease comes. I don't want to become an old man, but it comes anyway. What is the reason that these things are coming by force, despite my desires to the contrary? If I am forced, what is that force and why am I under this force? Who is enforcing these things? These things I do not know, but these are the real problems. I don't want excessive heat, but there is excessive heat. I have to take shelter of electric technology—a refrigerator, a cooler. Why? Who is enforcing these things? Why are they being enforced? I don't want this heat; what have I done? These are real questions, not just the study of foliage and writing volumes of books. That is a waste of energy. *Study yourself.* You don't want suffering, but why is it forced upon you? Who is enforcing? Why am I forced? These things you do not know.

Dr. Benford: Is it worthwhile, then, to try to stop excessive heat, say, or disease?

Śrīla Prabhupāda: You may want to stop the heat, but you cannot. Your scientific knowledge is not so perfect that you can stop the heat. Therefore, somebody is enforcing this. This is the right subject matter for thinking: Why am I being forced? Who is the enforcer? I don't want this heat, therefore I shall make an air conditioner. But this is only a temporary arrangement. You are scientifically advanced enough to manufacture nice medicine, so why can't you stop disease?

Dr. Benford: We don't understand it well enough.

Śrīla Prabhupāda: Therefore you are a fool. As soon as you don't understand, you are a fool.

Dr. Benford: Can you stop yourself from being an old man?

Śrīla Prabhupāda: Not immediately, but we are undergoing the process to stop it. Just like a man who is being treated for some disease—he is still suffering, but the fact that he is being treated means that he is going to stop it.

Dr. Benford: Well, that is our aim also. We would like to stop disease and even stop death.

Śrīla Prabhupāda: Everyone would like to, but you are not practicing the real procedure for stopping it.

Dr. Benford: But I don't want to suffer. Why is this necessary?

Śrīla Prabhupāda: It is because of the laws of nature. We are stealing from Kṛṣṇa, trying to enjoy independently of Kṛṣṇa. Therefore we are being punished by the laws of nature. It is not that Kṛṣṇa wants us to suffer. He does not like to punish us, but it is necessary in order to reform our character. A thief does not very much appreciate the police department, and he is thinking, "Why do they stop me from stealing?" But it is required. The government knows that the police department is necessary in order to curb the thieves and rogues. Although the thieves may not like it, the police department is nevertheless perfect. It is required.

Devotee: But why can't the police department just explain to the thief what he is doing wrong?

Śrīla Prabhupāda: Because he is a rascal. He will not listen. Law and order are for everyone, and to keep the citizens in order the police department is necessary. When a policeman at an intersection signals the traffic to stop, everyone must stop. He is not a highly placed officer, but because he is the representative of the government, you must stop, even if you are a very rich and important man. That is law and order, and everyone must obey. Similarly, the laws of nature are enforced by the demigods as representatives of Kṛṣṇa. Everyone must obey or be punished. You may not like it, but it is the law. Therefore there is so much pain.

Dr. Benford: Well, then, why is all this happening? What are we trying to attain? Why are we going through so much pain?

Śrīla Prabhupāda: Because you are not advancing beyond the bodily conception of life. You are simply advancing from one pain to another pain. But if you want to get out of pain, then you have to take to Kṛṣṇa consciousness and surrender to Kṛṣṇa. That is our proposition: Don't suffer pain after pain; stop it and surrender to Kṛṣṇa. That is our proposition. Everyone is trying to stop pain, both animals and man, in science and in ordinary work also. That is the real struggle. There is pain, and the struggle is to stop pain. And people take this struggle as happiness. But real happiness, real ecstasy, permanent ecstasy is there in the spiritual world, where there is no pain. This material happiness is called *māyā,* or illusion. Actually, people are not happy.

Dr. Benford: Why does a person like me, who is trying to understand the world rationally, find no way in which to do so?

Śrīla Prabhupāda: Yes, you are trying to know the world rationally, but you are not going to the proper teacher.

Dr. Benford: There are learned men in the world who simply study nature.

Śrīla Prabhupāda: Still, you require an experienced teacher. Of course, you can learn anything from nature, but not everyone is so intelligent that he can study nature properly. For example, if you study nature, why do you speculate that everything is void after death? Nature is not void—it is full of varieties. Therefore your study of nature is imperfect. Nature is not void, for we are sitting here surrounded by varieties—varieties of flowers, varieties of leaves, varieties of plants. If you say that nature is void, then your study of nature is not perfect.

Dr. Benford: I guess we don't understand it yet.

Śrīla Prabhupāda: That is your ignorance, but you cannot say it is void.

Dr. Benford: Well, we feel that our—

Śrīla Prabhupāda: *You* feel, *you* feel, but not others. Don't say "we."

Dr. Benford: We scientists.

Śrīla Prabhupāda: But there are other scientists who understand things differently. You are not the only scientists.

Dr. Benford: But I feel that if I study the world, there is a way to check my conclusions. You study the world and you think that you understand the physical process, and then you perform experiments, you verify your ideas, and then you see if you can apply the physical process in the world.

Śrīla Prabhupāda: That is another ignorance, because you do not know that you are imperfect.

Dr. Benford: Oh, I know that I am not perfect.

Śrīla Prabhupāda: Then what is the use of your researching in this way? If you are imperfect, the result will also be imperfect.

Dr. Benford: That's true.

Śrīla Prabhupāda: Yes. So why waste your time in this way?

Dr. Benford: But there doesn't seem to be any other way of finding knowledge.

Śrīla Prabhupāda: Therefore you have to approach the right teacher, who will show you. In order to become a scientist you have to go to the university and find a professor who can instruct you.

Dr. Benford: I could have done it by reading books.

Śrīla Prabhupāda: But a teacher is required also, or you cannot get your degree. Is it not?

Dr. Benford: Yes.

Śrīla Prabhupāda: So, when you want to learn something, you have to approach a teacher, and if the teacher is perfect, then you get perfect knowledge. This is the process. If the teacher is only another rascal like you, then whatever knowledge he may give you is useless. The teacher must be perfect; he must have real knowledge. Then he can teach. Therefore, the process is that you have to find out a perfect teacher. If you are fortunate, and you get such a perfect teacher, then you can learn everything. But if you approach a teacher who is as blind as you are, then you don't learn anything.

Dr. Benford: Are there many perfect teachers?

Śrīla Prabhupāda: Yes. Otherwise, there is no question of accepting a teacher. The first perfect teacher is Kṛṣṇa, and others are those who have learned from Him. For example, you are a scientist. Suppose I learn something from you. Even if I am not a scientist, because I have learned from you my knowledge is perfectly scientific.

Dr. Benford: I don't understand.

Śrīla Prabhupāda: Suppose a child goes to a mathematics teacher, and he says, ''Two plus two equals four.'' The child is not a mathematician, but if he accepts the teacher's teaching, "Two plus two equals four," and repeats that, then his knowledge is perfect.

Dr. Benford: But how does one know when the teacher is perfect? It seems to be very difficult.

Śrīla Prabhupāda: No, it is not difficult. A teacher is perfect who has learned from a perfect teacher.

Dr. Benford: But that merely removes the problem a step.

Śrīla Prabhupāda: No, it is not a problem. There is a perfect teacher, Kṛṣṇa, who is accepted by all classes of teachers as their teacher. In India, the Vedic civilization is conducted by Vedic teachers. All these Vedic teachers accept Kṛṣṇa as the supreme teacher. They take lessons from Kṛṣṇa, and they teach the same message. That is the process.

Dr. Benford: So everyone I might meet who accepts Kṛṣṇa as the perfect teacher is the perfect teacher?

Śrīla Prabhupāda: Yes, because he is teaching only Kṛṣṇa's teachings, that's all. It is the same as the example we gave before: they may not be personally perfect, but whatever they are speaking is perfect because it is taught by Kṛṣṇa.

Dr. Benford: Then you are not perfect.

Śrīla Prabhupāda: No, I am not perfect. None of us claims to be perfect; we have so many faults. But because we don't speak anything beyond Kṛṣṇa's teachings, our teaching is therefore perfect. For example, the postman may deliver to you a money order for one thousand dollars. He may not be a rich man, but if he simply delivers the envelope to you, you can cash the money order and be benefited. He may not be a rich man, but his dealings as a postman are perfect, because although he is not rich he can give you the thousand dollars. Similarly, our quality is that we are not perfect. We are full of imperfections, but we don't go beyond the teachings of Kṛṣṇa. That is our process. Like the same example we have given before: this small child is not a mathematician, but because he takes the teaching of a perfect mathematics teacher, "Two plus two equals four," his presentation is also perfect: "Two plus two equals four."

Dr. Benford: Why has Kṛṣṇa not told you everything about Himself?

Śrīla Prabhupāda: He has told everything; *everything* He has told. If you will study the *Bhagavad-gītā,* everything is there.

Dr. Benford: Well, if everything is there, why are we learning things we never knew before? I am speaking purely of science now. Why is science not written in the *Bhagavad-gītā?*

Śrīla Prabhupāda: Therefore, that so-called science is foolish. That is the conclusion. Actually, material science is foolish. The scientists are in darkness about so many things. What good is your science? There are so many things they do not know. In spite of all their imperfections they are claiming to have perfect knowledge. That is another foolishness.

Dr. Benford: Does it bother you that—

Śrīla Prabhupāda: We don't bother with the scientists. We simply take instruction from Kṛṣṇa. We have no business to take anything from the scientists. I don't decry your scientific discoveries. We welcome you. You are a scientist, and we appreciate your labor. But we criticize you only because you forget Kṛṣṇa. That is your problem. At the present moment your value is zero. Otherwise, if you remember Kṛṣṇa, when Kṛṣṇa is added you become 10, which is unlimitedly more valuable. That is the verdict of Nārada Muni:

> *idaṁ hi puṁsas tapasaḥ śrutasya vā*
> *sviṣṭasya sūktasya ca buddhi-dattayoḥ*
> *avicyuto 'rthaḥ kavibhir nirūpito*
> *yad-uttamaśloka-guṇānuvarṇanam*

"Learned circles have positively concluded that the infallible purpose of the advancement of knowledge—namely austerities, study of the *Vedas,* sacrifice, chanting of hymns, and charity—culminates in the transcendental descriptions of the Lord, who is defined in choice poetry." [*Śrīmad-Bhāgavatam* 1.5.22] Now, you are a scientist—physicist or chemist?

Dr. Benford: Physical.

Śrīla Prabhupāda: So, by your study of physical laws, if you try to prove there is God, that is your success.

Dr. Benford: It can't be done.

Śrīla Prabhupāda: Then that is your imperfection. You are a physicist, and as I said, if by your physical laws you can prove there is Kṛṣṇa, then you are perfect. You would give better service than we give. When we speak of Kṛṣṇa, there are so many persons who take our statements as sentimental religion. But if a scientist like you would speak of Kṛṣṇa, they would hear. If you do this, you will do greater service than I. But if it is a fact that by your physical laws you cannot understand Kṛṣṇa, then your science is imperfect. When you can come to understand Kṛṣṇa by studying these physical laws, then your science is perfect. Because He is the ultimate source of everything, if you can come to Kṛṣṇa by studying your physical laws, that is your perfection. Therefore, our proposition is that you remain a physical scientist, but you should try to explain Kṛṣṇa. Then you will be perfect. Don't think that we are decrying you or that we are decrying science. No. We are simply insisting that you accept Kṛṣṇa. Otherwise, you are zero. You have no spiritual value. Kṛṣṇa is like 1, and if you accept Kṛṣṇa, your value instantly becomes 10—unlimitedly increased. So, bring Kṛṣṇa into everything, and He will increase its value. That is real scientific discovery—to find out Kṛṣṇa. Find out how God is working in the physical and chemical laws, how His brain is working. Everything is working by His brain. There are chemical and physical energies, but everything is going on by God's brain. These chemical and physical laws are acting in such a subtle way that we see everything as coming automatically. There are chemical and physical laws, but how these laws are working you do not know.

Dr. Benford: We do not know why the laws are as they are.

Śrīla Prabhupāda: No, but Kṛṣṇa knows. Therefore, He is the creator. That is the difference between you and Kṛṣṇa. Kṛṣṇa can create a seed, a small seed the size of a mustard seed, and within that seed there is the potency to create a big banyan tree. That is also chemical composition, but you cannot do it. That is Kṛṣṇa's brain . . . that is Kṛṣṇa's brain.

Dr. Benford: But neither can you.

Śrīla Prabhupāda: No, I cannot. I have already said that I am imperfect. I do not claim unnecessarily that I am perfect. But I can say that the seed is created by Kṛṣṇa, and *that* you cannot do. That I can say. I can challenge you, that you cannot make this seed. Although I am imperfect, I can challenge you.

Dr. Benford: Essentially, however, you only know these things to be true because you have been told.

Śrīla Prabhupāda: Yes, that is required. Therefore, our Vedic knowledge is called *śruti. Śruti* means "that which is heard."

Dr. Benford: Then you cannot find out anything about Kṛṣṇa by studying science?

Śrīla Prabhupāda: There is nothing but Kṛṣṇa. There is nothing else except Kṛṣṇa.

Dr. Benford: But if we study the physical world, we study the work of Kṛṣṇa.

Śrīla Prabhupāda: Yes, but you don't know Kṛṣṇa. You don't say, as a rule, that you are studying the work of Kṛṣṇa, because you don't know Kṛṣṇa. You avoid Kṛṣṇa.

Dr. Benford: But Kṛṣṇa made it.

Śrīla Prabhupāda: Yes, that's a fact, but you do not know Kṛṣṇa. You simply know the grass. But I know the grass and Kṛṣṇa both. Therefore I am better than you.

Dr. Benford: Then we cannot find anything out about Kṛṣṇa by simply studying the grass?

Śrīla Prabhupāda: Then you are limited to grass, and know nothing beyond that.

Dr. Benford: Limited it may be, but is it not true?

Śrīla Prabhupāda: It is true, but limited, relative truth. In the *Vedānta-sūtra* the first statement is *athāto brahma-jijñāsā:* "Now, in this human form of life, let us inquire about the origin of everything." Not to study the relative truth, but the Absolute Truth—that is the business of the human form of life.

Dr. Benford: But how do I know this is true?

Śrīla Prabhupāda: That you have to learn from the teacher. That is the process.

Dr. Benford: But how do I know the teacher knows what is true?

Śrīla Prabhupāda: That knowledge is also available. When you wanted to learn science, what did you do? You found out a suitable teacher. If you can find a competent teacher, then everything can be understood.

Dr. Benford: But can the teacher demonstrate what he says to be true by experiment?

Śrīla Prabhupāda: Yes, everything can be demonstrated by experiment—everything.

Dr. Benford: But you cannot demonstrate things about Kṛṣṇa by experiment.

Śrīla Prabhupāda: Yes, it can be demonstrated. It *is* demonstrated. When you get a seed and sow it, a big tree comes from the seed. This is demonstration. How can you say it is not demonstration?

Dr. Benford: It is demonstration that a seed grows.

Śrīla Prabhupāda: Yes, the seed is the cause and the tree is the effect. That is demonstration.

Dr. Benford: But where's Kṛṣṇa?

Śrīla Prabhupāda: Kṛṣṇa says, "I am the seed." The seed is Kṛṣṇa. *Bījaṁ māṁ sarva-bhūtānām:* "I am the original seed of all existences." [Bg. 7.10] As soon as we see the seed, we see Kṛṣṇa. Kṛṣṇa says, "I am the seed." So how can you say you cannot see Kṛṣṇa? You can see Kṛṣṇa.

Dr. Benford: It's true we see mystery in the world.

Śrīla Prabhupāda: It is not mystery; it is fact. Kṛṣṇa says, "I am the seed." I have heard it from Kṛṣṇa. Therefore, when I see a seed I am seeing Kṛṣṇa. How can you say you are not perceiving Kṛṣṇa? You see Kṛṣṇa according to Kṛṣṇa's direction. Why do you persist in trying to see Kṛṣṇa in your own way? Kṛṣṇa says, *prabhāsmi śaśi-sūryayoḥ:* "I am the light of the sun and moon." [Bg. 7.10] As soon as you see the sunshine, you are seeing Kṛṣṇa. Why do you say you don't see Kṛṣṇa? What is your reason?

Dr. Benford: I do not know that it is called "Kṛṣṇa." I do not know—

Śrīla Prabhupāda: There are so many things you do not know. Therefore you have to learn from the teacher, Kṛṣṇa. Because you do not know and you do not care for Kṛṣṇa, therefore your knowledge is imperfect. This is your mentality. First of all, you do not know, and second, you do not accept Kṛṣṇa as your teacher. Do you think that your knowledge is perfect? What is the value of your knowledge?

Dr. Benford: But I do not know that there is any perfect knowledge.

Śrīla Prabhupāda: You do not know so many things, but we can know, because we accept Kṛṣṇa as our teacher.

Dr. Benford: The thing that bothers me most is that it seems to be necessary to accept things blindly.

Śrīla Prabhupāda: Yes, because our brains are imperfect. The child, when he is learning mathematics from his teacher, has no power to question or to protest. How has two plus two become four? He doesn't inquire. He simply accepts and becomes learned. That is the process. You cannot ask how Kṛṣṇa has made this seed, what is the chemical arrangement, the complete arrangement, so that the tree is coming out. It is coming out whether you understand or not. Therefore, you know that Kṛṣṇa is perfect. You cannot ask how the tree is coming out, nor is it within your power to understand how it is coming out. That is Kṛṣṇa's power. You scientists are just like children. The child is asking, "How is it that from this tape recorder so many sounds are coming out?" He cannot understand it. It is useless for him to try to understand it at the present stage of his development. But it is a fact that behind the mechanical arrangement of the tape recorder is a big science and a big brain. Similarly, the seed is undoubtedly a wonderful arrangement. Even though you do not understand—cannot understand—how a big tree is coming out from a tiny seed, still it is wonderful. And there is a brain, a wonderful brain, behind all this. That you have to accept.

So, the main business of human life is to understand Kṛṣṇa. For that purpose there must be scientific method and understanding—then human society is perfect. That is our propaganda. We do not say that you must accept religion and God by sentiment. No, accept it through philosophical and scientific inquiry. That is our propaganda. You shouldn't be a sentimental fanatic and accept blindly. You should try to understand this science of Kṛṣṇa consciousness.

So, I'm very glad to meet you, Dr. Benford. I want all scientists and philosophers to try to understand Kṛṣṇa in their own way. That will be the perfection of their learning. You are a real scientist when you explain Kṛṣṇa scientifically. That is your perfection.

Dr. Benford: I came today because I wanted to see if there is any similarity between your teachings and the findings of physics.

Śrīla Prabhupāda: That you will learn if you associate with us. Svarūpa Dāmodara, here, is also a scientist, and he's now learning the science of Kṛṣṇa consciousness. Now you cannot deviate him from Kṛṣṇa consciousness; he's become firmly convinced. Yet he's also a bona fide scientist—he's not a fool or a fanatic. Similarly, any reasonable scientist can understand Kṛṣṇa consciousness. Those who are dogmatic cannot understand, but those who follow our arguments— they will understand Kṛṣṇa consciousness. It is not difficult. We have books; we are not simply talking. We have dozens of books to help you understand.

Dr. Benford: As far as I can see, the universe is a thing that is striving to understand itself, and we are products of that attempt.

Śrīla Prabhupāda: No. "We" means the body. The body is a product of this universe, and the universe is a product of Kṛṣṇa. Therefore, the universe is not separate from Kṛṣṇa. The universe is also Kṛṣṇa. So, when you explain universal laws with reference to Kṛṣṇa, then it is perfect knowledge. The universe is one of Kṛṣṇa's energies—the material energy. We living entities are also an energy of Kṛṣṇa—the living energy. The combination of the living energy and the material energy—that is the universe. So, in one sense the study of the universe is also the study of Kṛṣṇa, but as long as you do not actually come to the point of understanding Kṛṣṇa, your knowledge is imperfect.

Gregory Benford is Associate Professor of Physics at the University of California, Irvine. He received his Ph.D. in theoretical physics from the University of California, San Diego, in 1967. He has published over forty scientific papers and has been a Woodrow Wilson Fellow. He was a Visiting Fellow at Cambridge University, England, in 1976. His research interests include solid-state physics, plasma physics, and high-energy astrophysics. His astronomical research centers on the dynamics of pulsars, violent extragalactic events, and quasars. He has also published numerous articles in *Natural History, Smithsonian, New Scientist,* and other major periodicals. His fiction includes several dozen short stories and three novels: *Jupiter Project* (1975), *If the Stars Are Gods* (1977), and *In the Ocean of Night* (1977). In 1975 he received the Nebula Award from the Science Fiction Writers of America for short fiction. He lives in Laguna Beach, California.

CHAPTER II

ON INSPIRATION

by Sadāpūta dāsa

In this article we will examine how human beings acquire knowledge in science, mathematics, and art. Our focus shall primarily be on the formation of ideas and hypotheses in science and mathematics, since the formal nature of these subjects tends to put the phenomena we are concerned with into particularly clear perspective. We will show that the phenomenon known as inspiration plays an essential part in acquiring knowledge in modern science and mathematics and the creative arts (such as music). We will argue that the phenomenon of inspiration cannot readily be explained by mechanistic models of nature consistent with present-day theories of physics and chemistry. As an alternative to these models, a theoretical framework for a nonmechanistic description of nature will be outlined. While providing a direct explanation of inspiration, this general framework is broad enough to include the current theories of physics as a limiting case.

Modern scientists acquire knowledge, at least in principle, by what is called the hypothetico-deductive method. Using this method, they formulate hypotheses and then test them by experimental observation. Investigators consider the hypotheses valid only insofar as they are consistent with the data obtained by observation, and they must in principle reject any hypothesis that disagrees with observation. Much analysis has been directed toward the deductive side of the hypothetico-deductive method, but the equally important process of hypothesis formation has been largely neglected. So we ask, "Where do the hypotheses come from?"

It is clear that scientists cannot use any direct, step-by-step process to derive hypothesis from raw observational data. To deal with such data at all, they must already have some working hypothesis, for otherwise the data amounts to nothing more than a bewildering array of symbols (or sights and sounds), which is no more meaningful than a table of random numbers. In this connection Albert Einstein once said, "It may be heuristically useful to keep in mind what one has observed. But on principle it is quite wrong to try grounding a theory on observable magnitudes alone. In reality the very opposite happens. It is the theory which determines what we can observe."[1]

Pure mathematics contains an equivalent of the hypothetico-deductive method. In this case, instead of hypotheses there are proposed systems of mathematical reasoning intended to answer specific mathematical questions. And instead of the experimental testing of a hypothesis there is the step-by-step process of verifying that a particular proof, or line of mathematical reasoning, is correct. This verification process is straightforward and could in principle be carried out by a computer. However, there is no systematic, step-by-step method of generating mathematical proofs and systems of ideas, such as group theory or the theory of Lebesque integration.

If hypotheses in science and systems of reasoning in mathematics are not generated by any systematic procedure, then what is their source? We find that they almost universally arise within the mind of the investigator by sudden inspiration. The classic example is Archimedes' discovery of the principle of specific gravity. The Greek mathematician was faced with the task of determining whether a king's crown was solid gold without drilling any holes in it. After a long period of fruitless endeavor, he received the answer to the problem by sudden inspiration while taking a bath.

Such inspirations generally occur suddenly and unexpectedly to persons who had previously made some unsuccessful conscious effort to solve the problem in question. They usually occur when one is not consciously thinking about the problem, and they often indicate an entirely new way of looking at it—a way the investigator had never even considered during his conscious efforts to find a solution. Generally, an inspiration appears as a sudden awareness of the problem's solution, accompanied by the conviction that the solution is correct and final. One perceives the solution in its entirety, though it may be quite long and complicated when written out in full.

Inspiration plays a striking and essential role in the solution of difficult problems in science and mathematics. Generally, investigators can successfully tackle only routine problems by conscious endeavor alone. Significant advances in science almost always involve sudden inspiration, as the lives of great scientists and mathematicians amply attest. A typical example is the experience of the nineteenth-century mathematician Karl Gauss. After trying unsuccessfully for years to prove a certain theorem about numbers, Gauss suddenly became aware of the solution. He described his experience as follows: "Finally, two days ago, I succeeded.... Like a sudden flash of lightning, the riddle happened to be solved. I myself cannot say what was the conducting thread which connected what I previously knew with what made my success possible."[2]

We can easily cite many similar examples of sudden inspiration. Here is another one, give by Henri Poincaré, a famous French mathematician of the late nineteenth century. After working for some time on certain problems in the theory of functions, Poincaré had occasion to go on a geological field trip, during which he set aside his mathematical work. While on the trip he received a sudden inspiration involving his researches, which he described as follows: "At the moment when I put my foot on the step the idea came to me, without anything in my former thoughts seeming to have paved the way for it, that the transformations I had used ... were identical with those of non-Euclidean geometry."[3] Later on, after some fruitless work on an apparently unrelated question, he suddenly realized, "with just the same characteristics of brevity, suddenness, and immediate certainty,"[1] that this work could be combined with his previous inspiration to provide a significant advance in his research on the theory of functions. Then a third sudden inspiration provided him with the final argument he needed to complete that work.

Although inspirations generally occur after a considerable period of intense but unsuccessful effort to consciously solve a problem, this is not always the case. Here is an example from another field of endeavor. Wolfgang Mozart once described how he created his musical works: "When I feel well and in good humor, or when I am taking a drive or walking, . . . thoughts crowd into my mind as easily as you could wish. Whence and how do they come? *I do not know and I have nothing to do with it. . . .* Once I have a theme, another melody comes, linking itself with the first one, in accordance with the needs of the composition as a whole. . . . Then my soul is on fire with inspiration, if however nothing occurs to distract my attention. The work grows; I keep expanding it, conceiving it more and more clearly until I have the entire composition finished in my head, though it may be long. . . . It does not come to me successively, with its various parts worked out in detail, as they will be later on, but it is in its entirety that my imagination lets me hear it."[5] (Italics added.)

From these instances we discover two significant features of the phenomenon of inspiration: first, its source lies beyond the subject's conscious perception; and second, it provides the subject with information unobtainable by any conscious effort. These features led Poincaré and his follower Hadamard to attribute inspiration to the action of an entity that Poincaré called "the subliminal self," and that he identified with the subconscious or unconscious self of the psychoanalysts. Poincaré came to the following interesting conclusions involving the subliminal self: "The subliminal self is in no way inferior to the conscious self; it is not purely automatic; it is capable of discernment; it has tact, delicacy; it knows how to choose, to divine. What do I say? It knows better how to divine than the conscious self, since it succeeds where that has failed. In a word, is not the subliminal self superior to the conscious self?"[6] Having raised this question, Poincaré then backs away from it: "Is this affirmative answer forced upon us by the facts I have just given? I confess that for my part, I should hate to accept it."[7] He then offers a mechanical explanation of how the subliminal self, viewed as an automaton, could account for the observed phenomena of inspiration.

The Mechanistic Explanation

Let us carefully examine the arguments for such a mechanical explanation of inspiration. This question is of particular importance at the present time, because the prevailing materialistic philosophy of modern science holds that the mind is nothing more than a machine, and that all mental phenomena, including consciousness, are nothing more than the products of mechanical interactions. The mental machine is specifically taken to be the brain, and its basic functional elements are believed to be the nerve cells and possibly some systems of interacting macromolecules within these cells. Many modern scientists believe that all brain activity results simply from the interaction of these elements according to the known laws of physics.

No one (as far as we are aware) has yet formulated an adequate explanation of the difference between a conscious and an unconscious machine, or even indicated how a machine could be conscious at all. In fact, investigators attempting to describe the self in mechanistic terms concentrate exclusively on the duplication of external behavior by mechanical means; they totally disregard each individual person's subjective experience of conscious self-awareness. This approach to the self is characteristic of modern behavioral psychology. It was formally set forth by the British mathematician A. M. Turing, who argued that since whatever a human being can do a computer can imitate, a human being is merely a machine.

For the moment we will follow this behavioristic approach and simply consider the question of how the phenomenon of inspiration could be duplicated by a machine. Poincaré proposed that the subliminal self must put together many combinations of mathematical symbols by chance until at last it finds a combination satisfying the desire of the conscious mind for a certain kind of mathematical result. He proposed that the conscious mind would remain unaware of the many useless and illogical combinations running through the subconscious, but that it would immediately become aware of a satisfactory combination as soon as it was formed. He therefore proposed that the subliminal self must be able to form enormous numbers of combinations in a short time, and that these could be evaluated subconsciously as they were formed, in accordance with the criteria for a satisfactory solution determined by the conscious mind.

As a first step in evaluating this model, let us estimate the number of combinations of symbols that could be generated within the brain within a reasonable period of time. A very generous upper limit on this number is given by the figure 3.2×10^{16}. We obtain this figure by assuming that in each cubic Angstrom unit of the brain a separate combination is formed and evaluated once during each billionth of a second over a period of one hundred years. Although this figure is an enormous overestimate of what the brain could possibly do within the bounds of our present understanding of the laws of nature, it is still infinitesimal compared to the total number of possible combinations of symbols one would have to form to have any chance of hitting a proof for a particular mathematical theorem of moderate difficulty.

If we attempt to elaborate a line of mathematical reasoning, we find that at each step there are many possible combinations of symbols we can write down, and thus we can think of a particular mathematical argument as a path through a tree possessing many successive levels of subdividing branches. This is illustrated in the figure below. The number of branches in such a tree grows exponentially with the number of successive choices, and the number of

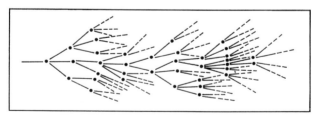

The relationship between different possible lines of mathematical reasoning can be represented by a tree. Each node represents a choice among various possibilities that restricts the further development of the argument.

choices is roughly proportional to the length of the argument. Thus as the length of the argument increases, the number of branches will very quickly pass such limits as 10^{16} and 10^{100} (1 followed by 100 zeros). For example, suppose we are writing sentences in some symbolic language, and the rules of grammar for that language allow us an average of two choices for each successive symbol. Then there will be approximately 10^{100} grammatical sentences of 333 symbols in length.

Even a very brief mathematical argument will often expand to great length when written out in full, and many mathematical proofs require pages and pages of highly condensed exposition, in which many essential steps are left for the reader to fill in. Thus there is only an extremely remote chance that an appropriate argument would appear as a random combination in Poincaré's mechanical model of the process of inspiration. Clearly, the phenomenon of inspiration requires a process of choice capable of going more or less directly to the solution, without even considering the vast majority of possible combinations of arguments.

Some Striking Examples

The requirements that this process of choice must meet are strikingly illustrated by some further examples of mathematical inspiration. It is very often found that the solution to a difficult mathematical problem depends on the discovery of basic principles and underlying systems of mathematical relationships. Only when these principles and systems are understood does the problem take on a tractable form; therefore difficult problems have often remained unsolved for many years, until mathematicians gradually developed various sophisticated ideas and methods of argument that made their solution possible. However, it is interesting to note that on some occasions sudden inspiration has completely circumvented this gradual process of development. There are several instances in which famous mathematicians have, without proof, stated mathematical results that later investigators proved only after elaborate systems of underlying relationships had gradually come to light. Here are two examples.

The first example concerns the zeta-function studied by the German mathematician Bernhard Riemann. At the time of his death, Riemann left a note describing several properties of this function that pertained to the theory of prime numbers. He did not indicate the proof of these properties, and many years elapsed before other mathematicians were able to prove all but one of them. The remaining question is still unsettled, though an immense amount of labor has been devoted to it over the last seventy-five years. Of the properties of the zeta-function that *have* been verified, the mathematician Jacques Hadamard said, "All these complements could be brought to Riemann's publication only by the help of facts which were completely unknown in his time; and, for one of the properties enunciated by him, it is hardly conceivable how he can have found it without using some of these general principles, no mention of which is made in his paper."[8]

The work of the French mathematician Evariste Galois provides us with a case similar to Riemann's. Galois is famous for a paper, written hurriedly in sketchy form just before his death, that completely revolutionized the subject of algebra. However, the example we are considering here concerns a theorem Galois stated, without proof, in a letter to a friend. According to Hadamard this theorem could not even be understood in terms of the mathematical knowledge of that time; it became comprehensible only years later, after the discovery of certain basic principles. Hadamard remarks "(1) that Galois must have conceived these principles in some way; (2) that they must have been unconscious in his mind, since he makes no allusion to them, though they by themselves represent a significant discovery."[9]

It would appear, then, that the process of choice underlying mathematical inspiration can make use of basic principles that are very elaborate and sophisticated and that are completely unknown to the conscious mind of the person involved. Some of the developments leading to the proof of some of Riemann's theorems are highly complex, requiring many pages (and even volumes) of highly abbreviated mathematical exposition. It is certainly hard to see how a mechanical process of trial and error, such as that described by Poincaré, could exploit such principles. On the other hand, if other, simpler solutions exist that avoid the use of such elaborate developments, they have remained unknown up to the present time, despite extensive research devoted to these topics.

The process of choice underlying mathematical inspiration must also make use of selection criteria that are exceedingly subtle and hard to define. Mathematical work of high quality cannot be evaluated simply by the application of cut-and-dried rules of logic. Rather, its evaluation involves emotional sensibility and the appreciation of beauty, harmony, and other delicate aesthetic qualities. Of these criteria Poincaré said, "It is almost impossible to state them precisely; they are felt rather than formulated."[10] This is also true of the criteria by which we judge artistic creations, such as musical compositions. These criteria are very real but at the same time very difficult to define precisely. Yet evidently they were fully incorporated in that mysterious process which provided Mozart with sophisticated musical compositions without any particular effort on his part and, indeed, without any knowledge of how it was all happening.

If the process underlying inspiration is not one of extensive trial and error, as Poincaré suggested, but rather one that depends mainly on direct choice, then we can explain it in terms of current mechanistic ideas only by positing the existence of a very powerful algorithm (a system of computational rules) built into the neural circuitry of the brain. However, it is not at all clear that we can satisfactorily explain inspiration by reference to such an algorithm. Here we will only briefly consider this hypothesis before going on to outline an alternative theoretical basis for the understanding of inspiration.

The brain-algorithm hypothesis gives rise to the following basic questions.

(1) *Origins.* If mathematical, scientific, and artistic inspirations result from the workings of a neural algorithm, then how does the pattern of nerve connections embodying this algorithm arise? We know that the algorithm cannot be a simple one when we consider the complexity of automatic

theorem-proving algorithms that have been produced thus far by workers in the field of artificial intelligence.[11] These algorithms cannot even approach the performance of advanced human minds, and yet they are extremely elaborate. But if our hypothetical brain-algorithm is extremely complex, how did it come into being? It can hardly be accounted for by extensive random genetic mutation or recombination in a single generation, for then the problem of random choice among vast numbers of possible combinations would again arise. One would therefore have to suppose that only a few relatively probable genetic transformations separated the genotype of Mozart from those of his parents, who, though talented, did not possess comparable musical ability.

However, it is not the general experience of those who work with algorithms that a few substitutions or recombinations of symbols can drastically improve an algorithm's performance or give it completely new capacities that would impress us as remarkable. Generally, if this were to happen with a particular algorithm, we would tend to suppose that it was a defective version of another algorithm originally designed to exhibit those capacities. This would imply that the algorithm for Mozart's unique musical abilities existed in a hidden form in the genes of his ancestors.

This brings us to the general problem of explaining the origin of human traits. According to the theory most widely accepted today, these traits were selected on the basis of the relative reproductive advantage they conferred on their possessors or their possessors' relatives. Most of the selection for our hypothetical hidden algorithms must have occurred in very early times, because of both the complexity of these algorithms and the fact that they are often carried in a hidden form. It is now thought that human society, during most of its existence, was on the level of hunters and gatherers, at best. It is quite hard to see how, in such societies, persons like Mozart or Gauss would ever have had the opportunity to fully exhibit their unusual abilities. But if they didn't, then the winnowing process that is posited by evolution theory could not effectively select these abilities.

We are thus faced with a dilemma: It appears that it is as

difficult to account for the origin of our hypothetical inspiration-generating algorithms as it is to account for the inspirations themselves.

(2) *Subjective experience.* If the phenomenon of inspiration is caused by the working of a neural algorithm, then why is it that an inspiration tends to occur as an abrupt realization of a complete solution, without the subject's conscious awareness of intermediate steps? The examples of Riemann and Galois show that some persons have obtained results in an apparently direct way, while others were able to verify these results only through a laborious process involving many intermediate stages. Normally, we solve relatively easy problems by a conscious, step-by-step process. Why, then, should inspired scientists, mathematicians, and artists remain unaware of important intermediate steps in the process of solving difficult problems or producing intricate works of art, and then become aware of the final solution or creation only during a brief experience of realization?

Thus we can see that the phenomenon of inspiration cannot readily be explained by means of mechanistic models of nature consistent with present-day theories of physics and chemistry. In the remainder of this article we will suggest an alternative to these models.

An Alternative Model

It has become fairly commonplace for scientists to look for correspondence between modern physics and ancient Eastern thought and to find intriguing suggestions for hypotheses in the *Upaniṣads,* the *Bhagavad-gītā,* and similar Vedic texts. The *Bhagavad-gītā* in particular gives a description of universal reality in which the phenomenon of inspiration falls naturally into place. Using some fundamental concepts presented in the *Bhagavad-gītā,* we shall therefore outline a theoretical framework for the description of nature that provides a direct explanation of inspiration, but that is still broad enough to include the current theories of physics as a limiting case. Since here we are offering these concepts only as subject matter for thought and discussion, we will not try to give a final or rigorous treatment.

The picture of universal reality presented in the *Bhagavad-gītā* differs from that of current scientific thinking in two fundamental respects.

(1) Consciousness is understood to be a fundamental feature of reality rather than a by-product of the combination of nonconscious entities.

(2) The ultimate causative principle underlying reality is understood to be unlimitedly complex, and to be the reservoir of unlimited organized forms and activities. Specifically, the *Bhagavad-gītā* posits that the underlying, absolute cause of all causes is a universal conscious being and that the manifestations of material energy are exhibitions of that being's conscious will. The individual subjective selves of living beings (such as ourselves) are understood to be minute parts of the absolute being that possess the same self-conscious nature. These minute conscious selves interact directly with the absolute being through consciousness, and they interact indirectly with matter through the agency of the absolute being's control of matter.

In modern science the idea of an ultimate cause underlying the phenomenal manifestation is expressed through the concept of the laws of nature. Thus in modern physics all causes and effects are thought to be reducible to the interaction of fundamental physical entities, in accordance with basic force laws. At the present moment the fundamental entities are thought by some physicists to comprise particles such as electrons, muons, neutrinos, and quarks, and the force laws are listed as strong, electromagnetic, weak, and gravitational. However, the history of science has shown that it would be unwise to consider these lists final. In the words of the physicist David Bohm, "The possibility is always open that there may exist an unlimited variety of additional properties, qualities, entities, systems, levels, etc., to which apply correspondingly new kinds of laws of nature."[12]

The picture of reality presented in the *Bhagavad-gītā* could be reconciled with the world view of modern physics if we were to consider mathematical descriptions of reality to be approximations, at best. According to this idea, as we try to formulate mathematical approximations closer and closer to reality, our formalism will necessarily diverge without limit in the direction of ever-increasing complexity. Many equations will exist that describe limited aspects of reality to varying degrees of accuracy, but there will be no single equation that sums up all principles of causation.

We may think of these equations as approximate laws of nature, representing standard principles adopted by the absolute being for the manifestation of the physical universe. The *Bhagavad-gītā* describes the absolute being in apparently paradoxical terms, as simultaneously a single entity and yet all-pervading in space and time. This conception, however, also applies to the laws of physics as scientists presently understand them, for each of these laws requires that a single principle (such as the principle of gravitational attraction with the universal constant G) apply uniformly throughout space and time.

The difference between the conceptions of modern physics and those presented in the *Bhagavad-gītā* lies in the manner in which the ultimate causal principle exhibits unity. The goal of many scientists has been to find some single, extremely simple equation that expresses all causal principles in a unified form. According to the *Bhagavad-gītā,* however, the unity of the absolute being transcends mathematical description. The absolute being is a single self-conscious entity possessing unlimited knowledge and potency. Therefore a mathematical account of this being would have to be limitlessly complex.

According to the *Bhagavad-gītā,* the phenomenon of inspiration results from the interaction between the all-pervading absolute being and the localized conscious selves. Since the absolute being's unlimited potency is available everywhere, it is possible for all varieties of artistic and mathematical creations to directly manifest within the mind of any individual. These creations become manifest by the will of the absolute being in accordance with both the desire of the individual living being and certain psychological laws.

Conclusion

We have observed that the attempt to give a mechanical explanation of inspiration based on the known principles of physics meets with two fundamental difficulties. First, the process of inspiration can be explained mechanically only if we posit the existence of an elaborate algorithm embodied in the neural circuitry of the brain. However, it is as hard to account for the origin of such an algorithm as it is to account for the inspirations themselves. Second, even if we accept the existence of such an algorithm, the mechanical picture provides us with no understanding of the subjective experience of inspiration, in which a person obtains the solution to a problem by sudden revelation, without any awareness of intermediate steps.

If it is indeed impossible to account for inspiration in terms of known causal principles, then it will be necessary to acquire some understanding of deeper causal principles operating in nature. Otherwise, no explanation of inspiration will be possible. It is here that the world view presented in the *Bhagavad-gītā* might be useful to investigators. The *Bhagavad-gītā* provides a detailed account of the laws by which the individual selves and the absolute being interact, and this account can serve as the basis for a deeper investigation of the phenomenology of inspiration.

References

1. S. G. Brush, "Should the History of Science Be Rated X?" *Science,* Vol. 183, p. 1167.

2. J. Hadamard, *The Psychology of Invention in the Mathematical Field* (Princeton: Princeton University Press, 1949), p. 15.

3. Henri Poincaré, *The Foundations of Science* (Lancaster, Pa.: The Science Press, 1946), pp. 387–88.

4. Ibid.

5. Hadamard, op. cit., p. 16.

6. Poincaré, op. cit., p. 390.

7. Ibid., p. 391.

8. Hadamard, op. cit., p. 118.

9. Ibid., p. 120.

10. Poincaré, op. cit., p. 390.

11. Joseph Weizenbaum, *Computer Power and Human Reason* (San Francisco: W. H. Freeman & Company, 1976), ch. 9.

12. David Bohm, *Causality and Chance in Modern Physics* (London: Routledge and Kegan Paul Ltd., 1957), p. 133.

CHAPTER III

THE COMPUTERIZED MR. JONES

by Sadāpūta dāsa

Science fiction writers often try to solve the problems of old age and death by taking advantage of the idea that a human being is essentially a complex machine. In a typical scene, doctors and technicians scan the head of the dying Samuel Jones with a "cerebroscope," a highly sensitive instrument that records in full detail the synaptic connections of the neurons in his brain. A computer then systematically transforms this information into a computer program that faithfully simulates that brain's particular pattern of internal activity.

When this program is run on a suitable computer, the actual personality of Mr. Jones seems to come to life through the medium of the machine. "I've escaped death!" the computer exults through its electronic phoneme generator. Scanning about the room with stereoscopically mounted TV cameras, the computerized "Mr. Jones" appears somewhat disoriented in his new embodiment. But when interviewed by old friends, "he" displays Mr. Jones's personal traits in complete detail. In the story, Mr. Jones lives again in the form of the computer. Now his only problem is figuring out how to avoid being erased from the computer's memory.

Although this story may seem fantastic, some of the most influential thinkers in the world of modern science take very seriously the basic principles behind it. In fact, researchers in the life sciences now almost universally assume that a living being is nothing more than a highly complex machine built from molecular components. In the fields of philosophy and psychology, this assumption leads to the inevitable conclusion that the mind involves nothing more than the biophysical functioning of the brain. According to this viewpoint, we can define in entirely mechanistic terms the words we normally apply to human personality—words like *consciousness, perception, meaning, purpose,* and *intelligence.*

Along with this line of thinking have always gone idle speculations about the construction of machines that can exhibit these traits of personality. But now things have gone beyond mere speculation. The advent of modern electronic computers has given us a new field of scientific investigation dedicated to actually building such machines. This is the field of artificial-intelligence research, or "cognitive engineering," in which scientists proceed on the assumption that digital computers of sufficient speed and complexity can in fact produce all aspects of conscious personality. Thus we learn in the 1979 M.I.T. college catalog that cognitive engineering involves an approach to the subjects of mind and intelligence that is "quite different from that of philosophers and psychologists, in that the cognitive engineer tries to produce intelligence."

In this article we shall examine the question of whether it is possible for a machine to possess a conscious self that perceives itself as seer and doer. Our thesis will be that while computers may in principle generate complex sequences of behavior comparable to those produced by human beings, computers cannot possess conscious awareness without the intervention of principles of nature higher than those known to modern science. Ironically, we can base strong arguments in support of this thesis on some of the very concepts that form the foundation of artificial-intelligence research. As far as computers are concerned, the most reasonable inference we can draw from these arguments is that computers cannot be conscious. When applied to the machine of the human brain, these arguments support an alternative, non-mechanistic understanding of the conscious self.

To begin, let us raise some questions about a hypothetical computer possessing intelligence and conscious self-awareness on a human level. This computer need not duplicate the mind of a particular human being, such as our Mr. Jones, but must simply experience an awareness of thoughts, feelings, and sensory perceptions comparable to our own.

First, let us briefly examine the internal organization of our sentient computer. Since it belongs to the species of digital computers, it consists of an information storehouse, or memory, an apparatus called the central processing unit (CPU), and various devices for exchanging information with the environment.

The memory is simply a passive medium used to record large amounts of information in the form of numbers. We can visualize a typical computer memory as a series of labeled boxes, each of which can store a number. Some of these boxes normally contain numerically coded instructions specifying the computer's program of activity. Others contain data of various kinds, and still others store the intermediate steps of calculations. These numbers can be represented physically in the memory as patterns of charges on microminiature capacitors, patterns of magnetization on small magnets, or in many other ways.

The CPU performs all the computer's active operations, which consist of a fixed number of simple operations of symbol manipulation. These operations typically involve the following steps: First, from a specified location (or "address") in the memory, the CPU obtains a coded instruction identifying the operation to be performed. According to this instruction, the CPU may obtain additional data from the memory. Then the CPU performs the operation itself. This may involve input (reading a number into the memory from an external device) or output (transmitting a number from the memory to an external device). Or the operation may involve transforming a number according to some simple rule, or shifting a number from one memory location to another. In any case, the final step of the operation will always involve the selection of a memory address where the next coded instruction is to be sought.

A computer's activity consists of nothing more than steps of this kind, performed one after another. The instruction codes stored in the passive memory specify the operations the CPU is to execute. The function of the CPU is simply to carry them out sequentially. The CPU's physical construction, like that of the memory, may include many kinds of components, ranging from microminiature semiconductor junctions to electromechanical relays. It is only the logical arrangement of these components, and not their particular physical constitution, that determines the functioning of the CPU.

Church's Thesis

We can most easily understand the operation of a computer by considering a simple example. Figure 1 illustrates a program of computer instructions for calculating the square root of a number.[1] The thirteen numbered statements correspond to the list of coded instructions stored in the com-

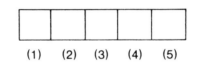

        (1)   (2)   (3)   (4)   (5)

1. Write 0 in (2).
2. Increment (2).
3. Write 0 in (3).
4. Copy (2) into (4).
5. If (4) equals 0, go to step 12.
6. Decrement (4).
7. Copy (2) into (5).
8. If (5) equals 0, go to step 5.
9. Decrement (5).
10. Increment (3).
11. Go to step 8.
12. If (3) is not greater than (1), go to step 2.
13. Decrement (2).

Fig. 1. Computer program for computing the square root of a number. To simulate the operation of the computer, place the number in box (1) and follow the instructions, starting with step 1. When step 13 is completed, the square root of the number (rounded down to an integer) will be in box (2). (In these instructions, "increment a number" means to add 1 to it, and "decrement a number" means to subtract 1 from it).

puter's memory. (Here, for clarity's sake, we have written them out in English.) The five boxes correspond to areas in the memory that store data and intermediate computational steps. To simulate the operation of the computer, place a number, such as 9, in box (1). Then simply follow the instructions. When you have completed the last instruction, the square root of your original number will be in box (2). In a computer, each of these instructions would be carried out by the CPU. They illustrate the kind of elementary operations used by present-day computers (although the operations do not correspond exactly to those of any particular computer).

The method of finding a square root given in our example may seem cumbersome and obscure, but it is typical of how computers operate. In fact, the practical applicability of computers rests on the observation that every fixed scheme of computation ever formulated can be reduced to a list of simple operations like the one in our example. This observation, first made by several mathematicians in the 1930s and '40s, is commonly known as Church's thesis. It implies that, in principle, any scheme of symbol manipulation we can precisely define can be carried out by a modern digital computer.

At this point, let us consider our hypothetical sentient computer. According to the exponents of artificial intelligence, the intricate behavior characteristic of a human being is nothing more than a highly complex scheme of symbol manipulation. Using Church's thesis, we can break down this scheme into a program of instructions comparable to our example in Figure 1. The only difference is that this program will be exceedingly long and complex—it may run to millions of steps. Of course, up till now no one has even come close to actually producing a formal symbolic description of human behavior. But for the sake of argument let's suppose such a description could be written and expressed as a computer program.

Now, assuming a computer is executing such a highly complex program, let us see what we can understand about the computer's possible states of consciousness. When executing the program, the computer's CPU will be carrying out only one instruction at any given time, and the millions of instructions comprising the rest of the program will exist only as an inactive record in the computer's memory. Now, intuitively it seems doubtful that a mere inactive record could have anything to do with consciousness. Where, then, does the computer's consciousness reside? At any given moment the CPU is simply performing some elementary operation, such as "Copy the number in box (1687002) into box (9994563)." In what way can we correlate this activity with the conscious perception of thoughts and feelings?

The researchers of artificial intelligence have an answer to this question, which they base on the idea of levels of organization in a computer program. We shall take a few paragraphs here to briefly explain and investigate this answer. First we shall need to know what is meant by "levels of organization." Therefore let us once again consider the simple computer program of Figure 1. Then we shall apply the concept of levels of organization to the program of our "sentient" computer and see what light this concept can shed on the relation between consciousness and the computer's internal physical states.

Levels of Organization

Although the square-root program of Figure 1 may appear to be a formless list of instructions, it actually possesses a definite structure, which is outlined in Figure 2. This structure consists of four levels of organization. On the highest level, the function of the program is described in a single sentence that uses the symbol *square root*. On the next level, the meaning of this symbol is defined by a description of the method the program uses to find square roots. This description makes use of the symbol *squared,* which is similarly defined on the next lower level in terms of another symbol, *sum.* Finally, the symbol *sum* is defined on the lowest level in terms of the combination of elementary operations actually used to compute sums in the program. Although for the sake of clarity we have used English sentences in Figure 2, the description on each level would normally use only symbols for elementary operations, or higher-order symbols defined on the next level down.

1. Find the **square root** of X.
2. The square root of X is one less than the first number Y with Y **squared** greater than X.
3. Y squared is the **sum** of Y copies of Y.
4. The sum of Y and another number is the result of incrementing that number Y times.

Fig. 2. Levels of organization of the program in Figure 1. The program in Figure 1 can be analyzed in terms of a hierarchy of abstract levels. The level of elementary operations is at the bottom, and each higher level makes use of symbols (such as *squared*) that are defined on the level beneath it.

These graded symbolic descriptions actually define the program, in the sense that if we begin with level 1 and expand each higher-order symbol in terms of its definition on a lower level, we will wind up writing the list of elementary operations in Figure 1. The descriptions are useful in that they provide an intelligible account of what happens in the program. Thus on one level we can say that numbers are being squared, on another level that they are being added, and on yet another that they are being incremented and decremented. But the levels of organization of the program are only abstract properties of the list of operations given in Figure 1. When a computer executes this program, these levels do not exist in any real sense, for the computer actually performs only the elementary operations in the list.

In fact, we can go further and point out that even this last statement is not strictly true, because what we call "the elementary operations" are themselves symbols, such as *Increment (3),* that refer to abstract properties of the computer's underlying machinery. When a computer operates, all that really happens is that matter and energy undergo certain transformations according to a pattern determined by the computer's physical structure.

In general, any computer program that performs some complex task can be resolved into a hierarchy of levels of description similar to the one given above. Researchers in artificial intelligence generally visualize their projected "intelligent" or "sentient" programs in terms of a hierarchy such as the following: On the bottom level they propose to describe the program in terms of elementary operations. Then come several successive levels involving mathematical procedures of greater and greater intricacy and sophistication. After this comes a level in which they hope to define symbols that refer to basic constituents of thoughts, feelings, and sensory perceptions. Next comes a series of levels involving more and more sophisticated mental features, culminating in the level of the ego, or self.

Here, then, is how artificial-intelligence researchers understand the relation between computer operations and consciousness: Consciousness is associated with a "sentient" program's higher levels of operation—levels on which symbolic transformations take place that directly correspond to higher sensory processes and the transformations of thoughts. On the other hand, the lower levels are not associated with consciousness. Their structure can be changed without affecting the consciousness of the computer, as long as the higher-level symbols are still given equivalent definitions. Referring again to our square-root program, we see that this idea is confirmed by the fact that the process of finding a square root given on level 2 in Figure 2 will remain essentially the same even if we define the operation of squaring on level 3 in some different but equivalent way.

If we were to adopt a strictly behavioristic use of the word *consciousness,* then this understanding of computerized consciousness might be satisfactory—granting, of course, that someone could indeed create a program with the required higher-order organization. Using such a criterion, we would designate certain patterns of behavior as "conscious" and others as not. Generally, a sequence of behavioral events would have to be quite long to qualify as "conscious." For example, a long speech may exhibit certain complex features that identify it as "conscious," but none of the words or short phrases that make it up would be long enough to display such features. Using such a criterion, one might want to designate a certain sequence of computer operations as "conscious" because it possesses certain abstract higher-order properties. Then one might analyze the overall behavior of the computer as "conscious" in terms of these properties, whereas any single elementary operation would be too short to qualify.

Defining Consciousness

We are interested, however, not in categorizing patterns of behavior as "conscious" or "unconscious" but rather in understanding the actual subjective experience of conscious awareness. To clearly distinguish this conception of consciousness from the behavioral one, we shall briefly pause here to describe it and establish its status as a subject of serious inquiry. By *consciousness* we mean the awareness of thoughts and sensations that we directly perceive and *know* that we perceive. Since other persons are similar to us, it is natural to suppose that they are similarly conscious. If this is accepted, then it follows that consciousness is an objectively existing feature of reality that tends to be associated with certain material structures, such as the bodies of living human beings.

Now, when a common person hears that a computer can be conscious, he naturally tends to interpret this statement in the sense we have just described. Thus he will imagine that a computer can have subjective, conscious experiences similar to his own. Certainly this is the idea behind such stories as the one with which we began this piece. One imagines the computerized "Mr. Jones," as he looks about the room through the computer's TV cameras, actually feeling astonishment at his strange transformation.

If the computerized Mr. Jones could indeed have such a subjective experience, then we would face the situation depicted in Figure 3. On the one hand, the conscious experience of the computer would exist—its subjective experience of colors, sounds, thoughts, and feelings would be an actual reality. On the other hand, the physical structures of the computer would exist. However, we cannot directly correlate consciousness with the actual physical processes of the computer, nor can we relate consciousness to the execution of individual elementary operations, such as those in Figure 1. According to the artificial-intelligence researchers,

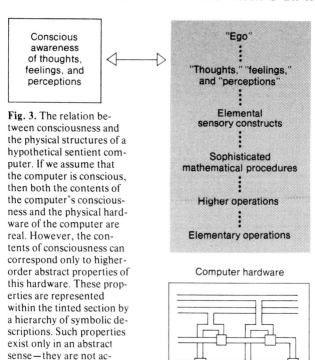

Conscious awareness of thoughts, feelings, and perceptions

"Ego"
⋮
"Thoughts," "feelings," and "perceptions"
⋮
Elemental sensory constructs
⋮
Sophisticated mathematical procedures
⋮
Higher operations
⋮
Elementary operations

Computer hardware

Fig. 3. The relation between consciousness and the physical structures of a hypothetical sentient computer. If we assume that the computer is conscious, then both the contents of the computer's consciousness and the physical hardware of the computer are real. However, the contents of consciousness can correspond only to higher-order abstract properties of this hardware. These properties are represented within the tinted section by a hierarchy of symbolic descriptions. Such properties exist only in an abstract sense—they are not actually present in the physical hardware of the computer.

consciousness should correspond to higher-order abstract properties of the computer's physical states—properties described by symbols such as *thought* and *feeling,* which stand at the top of a lofty pyramid of abstract definitions. Indeed, these abstract properties are the only conceivable features of our sentient computer that could have any direct correlation with the contents of consciousness.

Since consciousness is real, however, and these abstract properties are not, we can conclude only that something must exist in nature that can somehow "read" these properties from the computer's physical states. This entity is represented in Figure 3 by the arrow connecting the real contents

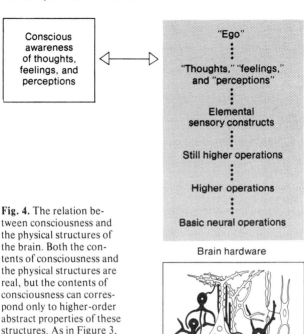

Fig. 4. The relation between consciousness and the physical structures of the brain. Both the contents of consciousness and the physical structures are real, but the contents of consciousness can correspond only to higher-order abstract properties of these structures. As in Figure 3, these properties are represented by the hierarchy of symbolic descriptions enclosed within the tinted section.

of consciousness with higher levels in the hierarchy of abstract symbolic descriptions of the sentient computer. The entity must have the following characteristics.

(1) It must possess sufficient powers of discrimination to recognize certain highly abstract patterns of organization in arrangements of matter.

(2) It must be able to establish a link between consciousness and such arrangements of matter. In particular, it must modify the contents of conscious experience in accordance with the changes these abstract properties undergo as time passes and the arrangements of matter are transformed.

There is clearly no place for an entity of this kind in our

current picture of what is going on in a computer. Indeed, we can conclude only that this entity must correspond to a feature of nature completely unknown to modern science.

This, then, is the conclusion forced upon us if we assume that a computer can be conscious. Of course, we can easily avoid this conclusion by supposing that no computer will ever be conscious, and this may indeed be the case. Aside from computers, however, what can we say about the relation between consciousness and the physical body in a human being? On one hand we know human beings possess consciousness, and on the other modern science teaches us that the human body is an extremely complex machine composed of molecular components. Can we arrive at an understanding of human consciousness that does not require the introduction of an entity of the kind described by statements (1) and (2)?

Ironically, if we try to base our understanding on modern scientific theory, then the answer is no. The reason is that all modern scientific attempts to understand human consciousness depend, directly or indirectly, on an analogy between the human brain and a computer. In fact, the scientific model for human consciousness is *machine* consciousness!

The Mechanical Brain

Modern scientists regard the brain as the seat of consciousness. They understand the brain to consist of many different kinds of cells, each a molecular machine. Of these, the nerve cells, or neurons, are known to exhibit electrochemical activities roughly analogous to those of the logical switching elements used in computer circuitry. Although scientists at present understand the brain's operation only vaguely, they generally conjecture that these neurons form an information-processing network equivalent to a computer's.

This conjecture naturally leads to the picture of the brain shown in Figure 4. Here thoughts, sensations, and feelings must correspond to higher levels of brain activity, which resemble the higher organizational levels of a complex computer program. Just as the higher levels of such a program are abstract, these higher levels of brain activity must also be abstract. They can have no actual existence, for all that actually happens in the brain is that certain physical processes take place, such as the pumping of sodium ions through neural cell walls. If we try to account for the existence of human consciousness in the context of this picture of the brain, we must conclude (by the same reasoning as before) that some entity described by statements (1) and (2) must exist to account for the connection between consciousness and abstract properties of brain states.

Furthermore, if we closely examine the current scientific world view, we can see that its conception of the brain as a computer does not depend merely on some superficial details of our understanding of the brain. Rather, on a deeper level, the conception follows necessarily from a mechanistic view of the world. Mechanistic explanations of phenomena are, by definition, based on systems of calculation. By Church's thesis, all systems of calculation can in principle be represented in terms of computer operations. In effect, all explanations of phenomena in the current scientific world view can be expressed in terms of either computer operations or some equivalent symbolic scheme.

This implies that all attempts to describe human consciousness within the basic framework of modern science must lead to the same problems we have encountered in our analysis of machine consciousness.[2] To account for consciousness, we shall inevitably require some entity like the one described in statements (1) and (2). Yet in the present theoretical system of science we find nothing, either in the brain or in a digital computer, that corresponds to this entity. Indeed, the present theoretical system could never provide for such an entity, for any mechanistic addition to the current picture of, say, the brain would simply constitute another part of that mechanistic system, and the need for an entity satisfying (1) and (2) would still arise.

Clearly, then, we must revise the basic theoretical approach of modern science if we are adequately to account for the nature of conscious beings. If we cannot do this in mechanistic terms, then we must adopt some other mode of scientific explanation. This brings us to the question of just what constitutes a scientific explanation.

A Nonmechanistic Explanation

Any theory intended to explain a phenomenon must make use of a variety of descriptive terms. We may define some of these terms by combining other terms of the theory, but there must inevitably be some terms, called primitive or fundamental, that we cannot so define. In a mechanistic theory, all the primitive terms correspond to numbers or arrangements of numbers, and scientists at present generally try to cast all their theories into this form. But a theory does not have to be mechanistic to qualify as scientific. It is perfectly valid to adopt the view that a theoretical explanation is scientific if it is logically consistent and if it enables us to deal practically with the phenomenon in question and enlarge our knowledge of it through direct experience. Such a scientific explanation may contain primitive terms that cannot be made to correspond to arrangements of numbers.

In our remaining space, we shall outline an alternative approach to the understanding of consciousness—an approach that is scientific in the sense we have described, but that is not mechanistic. Known as *sanātana-dharma*, this approach is expounded in India's ancient Vedic literatures, such as *Bhagavad-gītā* and *Śrīmad-Bhāgavatam*. We shall give a short description of *sanātana-dharma* and show how it satisfactorily accounts for the connection between consciousness and mechanism. This account is, in fact, based on the kind of entities described in statements (1) and (2), and *sanātana-dharma* very clearly and precisely describes the nature of these entities. Finally, we shall briefly indicate how this system of thought can enlarge our understanding of consciousness by opening up new realms of practical experience.

By accepting conscious personality as the irreducible basis of reality, *sanātana-dharma* departs radically from the mechanistic viewpoint. For those who subscribe to this viewpoint, all descriptions of reality ultimately boil down to combinations of simple, numerically representable entities, such as the particles and fields of physics. *Sanātana-dharma,* on the other hand, teaches that the ultimate foundation of reality is an Absolute Personality, who can be referred to by many personal names, such as Kṛṣṇa and Govinda. This primordial person fully possesses consciousness, senses, intelligence, will, and all other personal faculties. According to *sanātana-dharma,* all of these attributes are absolute, and it is not possible to reduce them to patterns of transformation of some impersonal substrate. Rather, all phenomena, both personal and impersonal, are manifestations of the energy of the Supreme Person, and we cannot fully understand these phenomena without referring to this original source.

The Supreme Person has two basic energies, the internal energy and the external energy. The external energy includes what is commonly known as matter and energy. It is the basis for all the forms and phenomena we perceive through our bodily senses, but it is insentient.

The internal energy, on the other hand, includes innumerable sentient beings called *ātmās.* Each *ātmā* is conscious and possesses all the attributes of a person, including senses, mind, and intelligence. These attributes are inherent features of the *ātmā,* and they are of the same irreducible nature as the corresponding attributes of the Supreme Person. The *ātmās* are atomic, individual personalities who cannot lose their identities, either through amalgamation into a larger whole or by division into parts.

Sanātana-dharma teaches that a living organism consists of an *ātmā* in association with a physical body composed of the external energy. *Bhagavad-gītā* describes the physical body as a machine, or *yantra,* and the *ātmā* as a passenger riding in this machine. When the *ātmā* is embodied, his natural senses are linked up with the physical information-processing system of the body, and thus he perceives the world through the bodily senses. The *ātmā* is the actual conscious self of the living being, and the body is simply an insentient vehiclelike mechanism.

If we refer back to our arguments involving machine consciousness, we can see that in the body the *ātmā* plays the role specified by statements (1) and (2). The *ātmā* is inherently conscious, and he possesses the sensory faculties and intelligence needed to interpret abstract properties of complex brain states. In fact, if we examine statements (1) and (2) we can see that they are not merely satisfied by the *ātmā;* they actually call for some similar kind of sentient, intelligent entity.

We can better understand the position of the *ātmā* as the conscious perceiver of the body by considering what happens when a person reads a book. When a person reads, he becomes aware of various thoughts and ideas corresponding to higher-order abstract properties of the arrangement of ink on the pages. Yet none of these abstract properties actually exists in the book itself, nor would we imagine that the book is conscious of what it records. As Figure 5 shows, to establish a correlation between the book on the one hand and conscious awareness of its contents on the other, there must be a conscious person with intelligence and senses who can read the book. Similarly, for conscious awareness to be associated with the abstract properties of states of a machine, there must be some sentient entity to read these states.

At this point one might object that if we try to explain a conscious person by positing the existence of another conscious person within his body, then we have actually explained nothing at all. One can then ask how the consciousness of *this* person is to be explained, and this leads to an infinite regress.

In response, we point out that this objection presupposes that an explanation of consciousness must be mechanistic. But our arguments about machine consciousness actually boil down to the observation that conscious personality cannot be explained mechanistically. An infinite regress of this kind is in fact unavoidable unless we either give up the effort to understand consciousness or posit the existence of a sentient entity that cannot be reduced to a combination of insentient parts. *Sanātana-dharma* regards conscious personality as fundamental and irreducible, and thus the "infinite regress" stops with the *ātmā.*

The real value of the concept of the *ātmā* as an explanation of consciousness is that it leads directly to further avenues of study and exploration. The very idea that the conscious self possesses its own inherent senses suggests that these senses should be able to function independently of the physical ap-

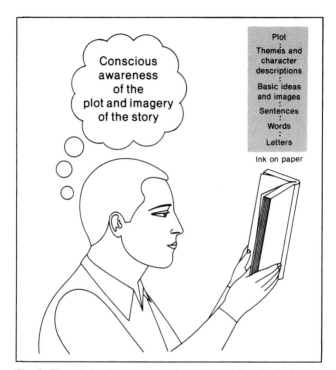

Fig. 5. The relation between consciousness and the physical structures of a book. When a person reads a book, he becomes aware of higher-order abstract properties of the patterns of ink on paper that are not directly present in these physical structures. One can similarly understand the correlation between consciousness and abstract properties of structures in Figure 4 if we posit the existence of a nonphysical agency with the sensory and cognitive faculties of a conscious person.

paratus of the body. In fact, according to *sanātana-dharma* the natural senses of the *ātmā* are indeed not limited to interpreting the physical states of the material brain. The *ātmā* can attain much higher levels of perception, and *sanātana-dharma* primarily deals with effective means whereby a person can realize these capacities in practice.

The Science of Consciousness

Since neither the Supreme Person nor the individual *ātmās* are combinations of material elements, it is not possible to scrutinize them directly through the material sensory apparatus. On the basis of material sensory information, we can only infer their existence by indirect arguments, such as the ones presented in this article. According to *sanātana-dharma*, however, we can directly observe and understand both the Supreme Person and the *ātmās* by taking advantage of the natural sensory faculties of the *ātmā*. Thus *sanātana-dharma* provides the basis for a true science of consciousness.

Since this science deals with the full potentialities of the *ātmā*, it necessarily ranges far beyond the realm of mechanistic thinking. When the *ātmā* is restricted to the physically embodied state, it can participate in personal activities only through the medium of machines, such as the brain, that generate behavior by the concatenation of impersonal operations. In this stultifying situation, the *ātmā* cannot manifest his full potential.

But the *ātmā* can achieve a higher state of activity, in which it participates directly in a relation of loving reciprocation with the Supreme Person, Kṛṣṇa. Since both the *ātmā* and Kṛṣṇa are by nature sentient and personal, this relationship involves the full use of all the faculties of perception, thought, feeling, and action. In fact, the direct reciprocal exchange between the *ātmā* and Kṛṣṇa defines the ultimate function and meaning of conscious personality, just as the interaction of an electron with an electric field might be said to define the ultimate meaning of electric charge. *Sanātana-dharma* teaches that the actual nature of consciousness can be understood by the *ātmā* only on this level of conscious activity.

Thus, *sanātana-dharma* provides us with an account of the nature of the conscious being that takes us far beyond the conceptions of the mechanistic world view. While supporting the idea that the body is a machine, this account maintains that the essence of conscious personality is to be found in an entity that interacts with this machine but is wholly distinct from it. Furthermore, one can know the true nature of this entity only in an absolute context completely transcending the domain of machines.

We have argued that the strictly mechanistic approach to life cannot satisfactorily explain consciousness. If we are to progress in this area, we clearly need some radically different approach, and we have briefly indicated how *sanātana-dharma* provides such an alternative. *Sanātana-dharma* explains the relationship between consciousness and machines by boldly positing that conscious personality is irreducible. It then goes on to elucidate the fundamental meaning of personal existence by opening up a higher realm of conscious activity—a realm that can be explored by direct experience. In contrast, the mechanistic world view can at best provide us with the sterile, behavioristic caricature of conscious personality epitomized by the computerized Mr. Jones.

Notes

1. In actual computer applications, much more sophisticated methods of calculating square roots would be used. The method presented in Figure 1 is intended to provide a simple example of the nature of computer programs.

2. For the sake of clarity, let us briefly indicate why this is so. Suppose one could describe a model of a sentient entity by means of a computer program. Then a certain level of organization of the program would correspond to the elementary constituents of the model. For example, in a quantum mechanical model these might be quantum wave functions. The level of the program corresponding to "thoughts" and "feelings" would be much higher than this level. Hence we conclude that this "cognitive" level would not in any sense exist in the actual system being modeled. It would correspond only to abstract properties of the states of this system, and thus an entity of the kind described in (1) and (2) would be needed to establish the association between the system and the contents of consciousness.

CHAPTER IV

THE PRINCIPLE OF REINCARNATION

by Bhaktisvarūpa Dāmodara Swami

The scientific study of reincarnation may shed new light on many subtle phenomena inexplicable by currently accepted theories—phenomena such as the wide variety of living forms, innate abilities clearly *not* acquired from the environment, and near-death experiences. In recent years scholars in various disciplines have shown great interest in studying reincarnation, but to study it meaningfully we must first know whether life is an eternal entity that transcends the temporary, physical body or merely a combination of molecules moving according to the laws of physics and chemistry.

The Reductionist Approach: Atoms and the Void

Modern science deals primarily with the objective aspects of nature. Relying on an experimental approach based on limited sensory data, it has pursued the goal of unfolding the hidden laws of nature, and ultimately of finding the original cause of the world we perceive. Most modern scientists now believe that blind physical laws and the laws of chance govern the cosmos. They say there is no designer, no creator, no God—no intelligence behind the whole cosmic phenomenon. Following this hypothesis, they attempt to reduce everything, including life, to the interactions of atoms and molecules, the familiar objects of study of physics and chemistry.

What Is Life?

Basing itself on a mountain of laboratory data, the currently predominant scientific theory holds that life is a coordinated chemical reaction. This theory involves the basic

assumption that the various life forms we see today origi-
nated by chance in an ancient chemical environment, the
"primordial soup," and that they have developed by the influence of chance and blind mechanical laws acting over a
long time period. In the words of Jacques Monod, "Chance
alone is at the source of every innovation, of all creation in
the biosphere. Pure chance, absolutely free but blind, is at
the very root of the stupendous edifice of evolution: this
central concept of modern biology is no longer one among
other possible or even conceivable hypotheses. It is today
the sole conceivable hypothesis, the only one that squares
with observed and tested fact."[1] This is the neo-Darwinian
concept. According to this idea, as time passed, the action of
various forms of energy (ultraviolet rays from the sun,
lightning, ionizing radiation, and heat) caused the small and
simple molecules to combine together to form the bio-
monomers (amino acids, for example), and these bio-
monomers in turn gave rise to biopolymers (such as
proteins and nucleic acids). It has been assumed that by the
proper interactions, the self-organization of these molecules
took place, and life eventually arose.

Unfortunately, this theory, however attractive it may be,
will remain only a theoretical model until its propounders
can actually produce some form of life in the laboratory by
chemical reactions. But just how likely is this? Assuming
that the primitive atmosphere was of a reducing kind,
Stanley Miller passed an electric discharge through a gaseous
mixture of ammonia, water vapor, carbon dioxide, and hydrogen.[2] The reaction product was found to contain
aldehydes, carboxylic acid, and some amino acids. Since
amino acids are the basic building blocks of protein
molecules, which in turn are the fundamental components
of living cells, Miller's experiment has been regarded as a
landmark in the case for chemicals' being the origin of life.
Subsequent experiments in the study of the origin of life involved some changes in the components of the reactants.
When the simple molecules of hydrogen cyanide (HCN)
were subjected to ultraviolet radiation, the basic building
blocks of nucleic acids (the purines adenine and guanine)
were synthesized. In experiments simulating the earth's

presumed primitive atmosphere, the simple molecules of formaldehyde (CH_2O) were generated, and these simple formaldehyde molecules in turn underwent various base-catalyzed condensation reactions to produce innumerable sugars. These are regarded as the progenitors of biological sugars. The action of ultraviolet light and ionizing radiation on solutions of formaldehyde produced the sugar molecules ribose and deoxyribose, which are the components of nucleic acids.

Practically speaking, then, at this stage of scientific knowledge most of the important chemicals found in the living cell (including the gene) can be synthesized in the chemical laboratory. And those in the forefront of microbiology and biochemistry have made a vigorous effort to put all the necessary chemicals together and prepare the first synthetic life in the test tube. Unfortunately, there are no life symptoms visible when all these chemicals are combined. Even without taking so much trouble to synthesize all these chemicals, scientists can actually isolate the necessary chemicals from an already living body and then recombine them. If life were a chemical combination, scientists could actually make life in the test tube by assembling all these important chemicals. They cannot do this, however. Thus there are abundant reasons for doubting that life is a chemical process.

Undoubtedly, in the last few decades great advancements have been made in the fields of cell biology, molecular biology, and biochemistry. Indeed, the discovery of the genetic code and many metabolic pathways of the living systems are products of brilliant and dedicated researchers. Because of the great successes of science and technology in many areas of human endeavor (medicine, agriculture, space science, and so on), inquisitive and enthusiastic scientific minds are tempted to believe that the brilliant ambition to synthesize life in the test tube will one day be fulfilled. Scientific and popular journals have thus reported many claims that certain molecular arrangements might give rise to life. They present, for example, the coacervate droplets of Oparin and the protenoid microspheres of Fox as forerunners of a living cell. But a close look at these entities reveals them to be purely physico-chemical phenomena.

Coacervate droplets are wholly explicable in the realm of micellar chemistry, and Fox's microspheres are explicable in terms of the chemistry of peptides and polypeptides.

Therefore, despite great scientific discoveries and achievements, the bright hope and enthusiasm for understanding life in molecular terms seem to be losing ground, and many prominent scientists in various fields are beginning to doubt the validity of this concept. In a book called *Biology Today,* Nobel-prize–winning chemist Albert Szent-Györgyi remarked, "In my search for the secret of life, I ended up with atoms and electrons, which have no life at all. Somewhere along the line, life ran out through my fingers. So, in my old age, I am now retracing my steps. . . ."[3]

Not only do molecules, atoms, and electrons lack life symptoms, but also the chemical view of life fails to correspond with life's observed subtleties—human beings' unique feeling, willing, and thinking capacities, for example. If life were an interplay of molecules, we should be able to explain these subtle aspects of life in terms of molecules only. What will be the genetic component or molecule that induces the friendly feeling of love and respect among people? Which molecule or genetic code will be responsible for the subtle artistic nuances in *Hamlet* or Bach's *Mass in B Minor*? Can a mechanistic view of life account for life's value- and goal-oriented nature, especially among human beings? That there are no plausible molecular mechanisms to explain these subtle aspects of life makes it reasonable to propose that *life transcends physics and chemistry.*

A New Paradigm for Life and the Absolute Truth

If life were accepted as a totally temporary, material phenomenon, then the idea of a previous or future life of a living being would be eliminated, and with it the question of reincarnation. Of course, as we have seen, there is every reason to believe that life *is* transcendental to matter and thus independent of the physico-chemical laws that govern matter. What we need now, to study reincarnation scientifically, is a new scientific paradigm that will explain the origin of life, its characteristics, and how it behaves in the world of matter.

Before discussing this new scientific paradigm, we will find it useful to briefly discuss the nature of the Absolute Truth. As mentioned earlier, according to modern science the Absolute Truth (defined as *"the ultimate cause of all phenomena"*) seems to be vaguely incorporated into the physical laws called the laws of nature. In other words, modern science posits the Absolute Truth as blind, impersonal, and wholly within the framework of the push-pull mechanisms of atoms and molecules. Now, if nature were simply an array of particles moving according to mathematical equations, it would be possible to predict events such as birth, death, accidents, and wars with the help of these equations. Indeed, it should be possible to understand all the intricacies of life—past, present, and future—in terms of mathematical equations. However, all careful thinkers, especially the scientists, know that this is impossible—that a purely mathematical approach to the understanding of life is too restrictive and very unsatisfying. Therefore we need a new paradigm for the origin and nature of life.

The new scientific paradigm we are proposing, which accounts for both the subtle complexities of life and the apparently nonphysical character of the Absolute Truth, comes basically from the scientific and theological background of the *Vedas*. According to the ancient wisdom outlined in the *Bhagavad-gītā* (a basic Vedic text), the Absolute Truth is the supreme person, possessing supreme consciousness and supreme intelligence. In other words, the Absolute Truth is a supremely sentient being. The Absolute Truth emanates two energies: the inferior energy, called *prakṛti* in Sanskrit and characterized by inanimate matter; and the superior energy, which is composed of *ātmās,* living entities. The *ātmās* are called the superior energy because they possess consciousness, which is the main feature that distinguishes life from matter.

The behavior of inanimate matter can be described to some extent in terms of the push-pull mechanisms operating on molecular, atomic, and subatomic levels, and these push-pull mechanisms can in turn be described by using simple mathematical equations. As we have already pointed out, however, there are no mathematical laws that can describe the phenomena of life and its variegated activities. Therefore, life is clearly transcendental to material laws and can be defined, according to the *Vedas,* as "*the nonphysical, fundamental particle called the* ātmā, *which is characterized by consciousness.*"

Since life is nonphysical and nonchemical, the mathematical laws that govern the activities of inert matter do not apply to life. However, it is reasonable to suppose that there must be *some* laws that govern life. According to the *Bhagavadgītā,* these are higher-order natural laws incorporating free will. (As we shall see, free will plays a very important role in reincarnation.) It is clear that the existing scientific models and tools cannot grasp these higher-order natural laws, but it is conceivable that the parapsychological experiments now underway in many quarters may provide at least some clue as to the nature of these laws. Thus there is a vast area for further research in the fields of parapsychology and psychology that may help us understand the science of life and its variegated activities.

The Properties of Life (the Ātmā)

There are innumerable *ātmās* (living entities), each being a quantum of consciousness. Each *ātmā* resides temporarily in an ephemeral biological form, according to the *ātmā's* consciousness. This consciousness is due to the *ātmā* alone, but the content of the *ātmā's* consciousness is due to its interactions with the particular body it occupies. The material body can be divided into two categories: the gross and the subtle. The subtle body is made up of mind, intelligence, and the apparent self (or the false identification of one's self with the material body). The gross body is made up of the five gross elements—solid matter, liquids, radiant energy, gases, and ethereal substances. The interaction of the individual *ātmā* with the gross and subtle bodies produces inconceivably complex reactions, which cannot be explained by simple chemistry and physics in the living cell. That is why chemistry and physics cannot explain why there is so much difference between a living body and a dead one. Simply put, when the individual living being leaves the body, the live body becomes dead matter—although all the chemicals necessary for the functioning of the living organism are still present.

Consciousness and the Biological Forms

According to the information given in the *Vedas*, the varieties of life forms are products of the combinations and permutations of the three modes of material nature (goodness, passion, and ignorance). The life forms are just like temporary houses or apartments of various sizes, shapes, and colors, in which the eternal self, or living being, resides temporarily. The biological forms, governed by the three modes, put a constraint on the qualities and activities of the living beings' consciousness. Thus the individual being in a tiger's body will roar loudly and kill animals for food, while the living being in a swan's body will fly gracefully and swim on the surface of lakes. Even in the same family we see differences caused by the activities of the three modes of nature. Although all animals are in the mode of ignorance, they are influenced by the modes of goodness and passion in varying degrees. Cows, for example, are very simple, and their behavior is very mild; they are influenced by the mode of goodness to some extent. The ferocious nature of lions and tigers, on the other hand, reveals their passionate consciousness, while camels are almost completely in the mode of ignorance. In a similar manner, in the family of birds the swans are very noble and gracious, showing symptoms of goodness; hawks, eagles, and peacocks are predominantly in the mode of passion; and vultures and crows are predominantly in the mode of ignorance. Although the biological forms in the same family are similar in nature, the consciousness and behavior of these birds and animals are different. Thus there are millions of forms where the eternal self, or living being, temporarily resides, displaying its behavior according to how the three modes of material nature affect its consciousness.

Reincarnation and the Change of Body

Now the question arises: "What determines the particular biological form and type of consciousness that a living being acquires?" To answer this question, let us first investigate the transformations of form and consciousness that occur within one lifetime.

As mentioned earlier, consciousness and biological form are interrelated, due to the influence of the modes of nature. Thus a child's body and its conscious development are different from those of its youthful stage, and so on. In principle, then, as the body changes from boyhood to old age, the living being, or *ātmā*, actually passes through many bodies of various ages and varieties of conscious development. Thus the body changes, but the eternal living being within the body—the self—remains the same. Biological science confirms this. In his book *The Human Brain*, John Pfeiffer points out, "Your body does not contain a single one of the molecules that it contained seven years ago." The movement of the living entity through numerous bodies within one lifetime—something we can all verify by a little introspection—can be termed *internal (or continuous) reincarnation or transmigration.*

But what about the living being's passage to a new body at the time of death? To the author's knowledge; reports in the literature on the study of reincarnation are based primarily on some scattered data regarding some children's memories of previous lives. This information comes mainly from northern India, Sri Lanka, Burma, Thailand, Vietnam, and some areas of western Asia.[1] Although this information certainly supports the theory of reincarnation, it does not provide us with a scientific foundation from which to study it, because the vast majority of people cannot remember their past lives. Therefore we must consult a source of information more reliable than haphazard memory. That information is available in the *Vedas*. In the *Bhagavad-gītā* Lord Kṛṣṇa very clearly explains reincarnation to His friend and devotee Arjuna. The Lord says, "Just as a person puts on new garments, giving up old ones, similarly the individual living entity accepts new material bodies, giving up the old

and useless ones." (Bg. 2.22) "Just as the embodied living
entity passes, in one body, from boyhood to youth to old
age, so the living entity similarly passes into another body at
death." (Bg. 2.13) Lord Kṛṣṇa further explains that the
mind is the mechanism underlying all these transmigrations:
"Whatever state of being one remembers when he quits his
body, that state he will attain without fail in his next life."
(Bg. 8.6) So, the living entity in a man's body could go into
the body of an animal, a bird, an insect, a plant, another
human, and so on. This journey of the self, or living entity,
into different bodies can be referred to as *external (or discontinuous) reincarnation or transmigration.*

To illustrate how external reincarnation works, we will
briefly relate the story of King Bharata, one of the great personalities in Vedic history, from the *Śrīmad-Bhāgavatam*, the
foremost of the eighteen *Purāṇas.*

One day, after King Bharata had taken his bath as
usual in the River Gaṇḍakī, he was chanting his *mantra*
when he saw a pregnant deer come to the riverbank to
drink water. Suddenly the thundering roar of a lion resounded throughout the forest. The deer was so
frightened that it immediately gave birth to its calf. It
crossed the river, but then died immediately thereafter.
Bharata took compassion on the motherless calf,
rescued it from the water, took it to his *āśrama*, and
cared for it affectionately. He gradually became attached
to the young deer, and he always thought of it lovingly.

As it grew up, the deer became Bharata's constant
companion, and he always took care of it. Gradually he
became so absorbed in thinking of this deer that his
mind became agitated, he reduced his meditative disciplines, and he fell away from his mystic *yoga* practice.
Once, when the deer was absent, Bharata was so disturbed that he began to search for it. While searching
and lamenting the deer's absence, Bharata fell down and
died. Because his mind was fully absorbed in thinking of
the deer, he naturally took his next birth in the womb of
a deer. (*Bhāg.* 5.8)

As has been mentioned earlier, there is a subtle body, made up of mind, intelligence, and apparent self. In either kind of reincarnation, internal or external, the living being is carried by the subtle body under the laws of *karma*. The word *karma* is a Sanskrit term that can be defined as "*the function and activity of the living entity within the framework of his free will and under the influence of the three modes of material nature over a span of time.*" For every action that an individual living being performs, he must undergo an appropriate reaction. For example, if someone is very charitable toward educational institutions, in his next life he may be very wealthy and receive an excellent education. On the other hand, if one performs or has an abortion, he or she will suffer the same fate in the next life. Thus we arrive at a definition of reincarnation, or transmigration, according to the Vedic information: "*the continuous journey of the living entity from one body to another, either internally or externally, under the stringent laws of his individual* karma."

Evolution and Devolution of Consciousness

Darwinian evolution, or in modern times chemical evolution, assumes that it is strictly the morphology of an organism that evolves. The Vedic literatures, however, give us the information that it is not the body that evolves but rather the living being's consciousness. And this evolution of consciousness takes place by the process of the living being's transmigration from one body to another. Those living entities that are below the human form of life never violate the laws of nature; they have no choice but to follow them. So their transmigration is strictly unidirectional—from less conscious forms to more conscious forms. Thus microbes, plants, birds, and animals all evolve until they reach the human form of life.

However, when the individual living being comes to the human form of life, his consciousness is fully developed, and along with it his free will. Thus the individual being in the human form can be obstinately rebellious against the laws of nature, or he can be completely harmonious with the laws of nature. In other words, he can exercise his free will either to evolve to a higher plane of consciousness or to revert to a lower stage. From the human form of life, if the individual living being desires, he can escape the continuous cycle of transmigration from one form of body to another. This can be done by using his free will properly. On the other hand, if he exercises his free will improperly, then he can go back to the lower species. And this is called devolution of consciousness—the passage of the living being from higher consciousness to lower consciousness—which intelligent men wish to avoid.

Reincarnation and the Science of Self-realization

The eternal wisdom of the *Vedas* instructs us that the goal of all knowledge is to break free from the repeated cycle of birth and death. The intelligence of all forms of life below human beings is insufficiently developed to understand the science of self-realization. Therefore the *Vedānta-sūtra* says that in the human form of life one must inquire into the nature of the Absolute Truth.

We must begin by asking such questions as these: "Who am I?" "Where do I come from?" "What is the purpose of my existence?" "How can I get out of the cycle of repeated birth and death?" We should investigate the answers to all these questions very thoroughly. This is the beginning of the science of self-realization, or the science of the study of life.

Bhakti-yoga: The Process for Breaking the Chain of Birth and Death

The systematic process for studying the self is called *bhakti-yoga*. *Bhakti-yoga* is, once again, a Sanskrit term meaning "*the spiritual discipline by which one links up with the Absolute Truth, the Supreme Person, in love.*" The basic tenet of *bhakti-yoga* is that in order to get accurate knowledge concerning the Absolute Truth, one must train the mind properly so that it is eligible to receive the knowledge coming from the higher source. We have already discussed how our new scientific paradigm describes the Absolute Truth as supremely sentient, and that everything—matter, life, knowledge, and so on—comes from that absolute source. In order to receive real knowledge, one's mind must be free from the contamination of the lower modes of nature. One of the main impurities is the false pride, or hubris, that impels us to believe we can understand everything by the process of experimental knowledge. We must give up this hubris, control the mind, and make it harmonious with nature. To control and train the mind, we must follow certain disciplines, one of the most basic of which is to hear proper sound vibrations. These sound vibrations are called *mantras,* which literally means "sound vibrations that can deliver the mind." The most important *mantra* given in the *Vedas* is the Hare Kṛṣṇa *mantra:* Hare Kṛṣṇa, Hare Kṛṣṇa, Kṛṣṇa Kṛṣṇa, Hare Hare/ Hare Rāma, Hare Rāma, Rāma Rāma, Hare Hare. Chanting this *mantra* regularly is the easiest and most effective method for purifying the mind of all influences of the lower modes of nature.

The gold we obtain from a gold mine is usually in a very impure state, but by a purificatory chemical process we can refine pure gold from it. Similarly, when the mind is contaminated by the material modes of nature, it becomes impure. We have to remove these impurities by chanting the Hare Kṛṣṇa *mantra.* Gradually our consciousness will become purer and purer, and our real identity will be revealed to us.

Thus, by developing pure consciousness we can revive our original identity as purely spiritual beings, uncontaminated by the modes of nature. In this stage we do not identify ourselves any longer with the body, gross or subtle, and we are on the plane of God consciousness, or Kṛṣṇa consciousness. Thus we are free of reincarnation once and for all.

References
1. Jacques Monod, *Chance and Necessity,* trans. Austryn Wainhouse (New York: Alfred A. Knopf, 1971), pp. 112–13.
2. Stanley Miller, *Science,* Vol. 117, No. 528 (1953).
3. Albert Szent-Györgyi, *Biology Today,* (Del mar, California: CRM Books, 1972).
4. Ian Stevenson, "The Explanatory Value of the Idea of Reincarnation," *The Journal of Nervous and Mental Disease,* Vol. 164 (1977), No. 5, p. 308.

About the Authors

His Divine Grace A. C. Bhaktivedanta Swami Prabhupāda was born in Calcutta, India, in 1896. After earning his degree at Scottish Churches' College, he met his spiritual master, Śrīla Bhaktisiddhānta Sarasvatī Ṭhākura, who requested him to spread the science of Kṛṣṇa consciousness to the Western people through the medium of the English language. In fulfillment of this order, Śrīla Prabhupāda came to America in 1965 and founded the International Society for Krishna Consciousness, which he molded into a worldwide confederation of *āśramas,* schools, temples, and farm communities. During his lifetime (1896–1977), Śrīla Prabhupāda wrote and published some seventy volumes of translations and commentaries on India's Vedic literature, which are now standard in universities around the world. In 1976, Śrīla Prabhupāda established the Bhaktivedanta Institute, composed of ISKCON members with advanced degrees in the sciences. The Institute is devoted to the study of the Vedic literatures and their relationship with modern science.

Bhaktisvarūpa Dāmodara Swami (Dr. T. D. Singh) was born in Manipur, India, in 1941. He received his B.S. with honors from Gauhati University, his Master of Technology degree with honors from Calcutta University, his M.S. in chemistry from Canisius College in Buffalo, New York, and in 1974 completed his Ph.D. in physical organic chemistry at the University of California at Irvine. His research interests include molecular biology, chemical evolution and the origins of life, the nature of consciousness, biomedical ethics, and the philosophy of science. He is currently a member of the American Chemical Society, the International Society for the Study of the Origin of Life, and the American Association for the Advancement of Science and is presently the director of the Bhaktivedanta Institute.

Sadāpūta dāsa, born in New York in 1947, received his B.S. in mathematics and physics from the State University of New York at Binghampton, his M.A. in mathematics from Syracuse University, and in 1974 received his Ph.D. in mathematics from Cornell University, where he specialized in probability theory. His research interests include information theory, quantum mechanics, mathematical models for the study of life, and the philosophy of science.

Questions and comments about the subject matter of this book can be sent to Sadāpūta dāsa at 72 Commonwealth Avenue, Boston, Massachusetts 02116.

ISKCON Centers
Around the World

ISKCON is a worldwide community of devotees dedicated to the principles
of *bhakti-yoga*. Write, call, or visit for further information.
Classes are held in the evenings during the week,
and a special feast and festival is held every Sunday afternoon.

AFRICA

Durban (Natal), S. Africa — P.O. Box 212, Cato Ridge, Natal 3680 / Cato Ridge 237; **Johannesburg, S. Africa** — Elberta Rd., Honeydew (mail: P.O. Box 5302, Weltevreden Park 1715) / 6752845; **Lagos, Nigeria** — P.O. Box 8793, West Africa; **Mauritius** — 10 E. Serret St., Rose Hill (mail: P.O. Box 718, Port Louis, Mauritius); **Mombasa, Kenya, E. Africa** — Madhavani House, Sauti Ya Kenya and Kisumu Rd., P.O. Box 82224 / 312248; **Nairobi, Kenya, E. Africa** — Puran Singh Close, P.O. Box 28946 / 331568.

ASIA

INDIA: Ahmedabad, Gujarat — 7, Kailas Society, Ashram Rd., 380 009 / 49935; **Bangalore, Mysore** — 34/A, 9B Cross. West of Chord Rd., Rajajinagar 2nd Stage, 560 010; **Bhadrak, Orissa** — Gour Gopal Mandir, Kuans, P.O. Bhadrak, Dist. Balasore; **Bhubaneswar, Orissa** — National Highway No. 5, Nayapalli (mail: c/o P.O. Box 173, 751 001) / 53125; **Bombay, Maharastra** — Hare Krishna Land, Juhu, 400 049 / 566-860; **Calcutta, W. Bengal** — 3 Albert Rd., 700 017 / 44-3757; **Chandigarh, Punjab** — Hare Krishna Land, Dakshin Marg, Sector 36-B, 160 023; **Chhaygharia (Haidaspur), W. Bengal** — Thakur Haridas Sripatbari Sevashram, P.O. Chhaygharia, P.S. Bongaon, Dist. 24 Parganas; **Gauhati, Assam** — Post Bag No. 127, 781 001; **Hyderabad, A.P.** — Hare Krishna Land, Nampally Station Rd., 500 001 / 51018; **Imphal, Manipur** — Paona Bazar, 795 001; **Madras, Tamil Nadu** — 4 Srinivasamurty Ave., Adayar, Madras 20; **Mayapur, W. Bengal** — Shree Mayapur Chandrodaya Mandir, P.O. Shree Mayapur Dham (District Nadia); **New Delhi, U.P.** — M-119 Greater Kailash 1, 110 048 / 624-590; **Patna, Bihar** — Post Bag 173, Patna 800 001; **Vrindavan, U.P.** — Krishna-Balarama Mandir, Bhaktivedanta Swami Marg, Raman Reti, Mathura / 178.

FARMS: Hyderabad, A.P. — P.O. Dabilpur Village, Medchal Taluq, Hyderabad District, 501 401; **Mayapur, W. Bengal** — (contact ISKCON Mayapur).

RESTAURANTS: Bombay — Hare Krishna Land; **Mayapur** — Shree Mayapur Chandrodaya Mandir; **Vrindavan** — Krishna-Balarama Mandir.

OTHER COUNTRIES: Bangkok, Thailand — P.O. Box 12-1108; **Butterworth, Malaysia** — 1 Lintang Melur, M.K. 14, Butterworth, Province Wellesley / 04-331019; **Colombo, Sri Lanka** — 188, New Chetty St., Colombo 13 / 33325; **Hong Kong** — 5 Homantin St., Flat 23, Kowloon / 3-029113; **Kathmandu, Nepal** — 8/6, Battis Putali, Goshalla; **Mandaue City, Philippines** — 231 Pagsabungan Rd., Basak, Cebu / 83254; **Saitama-Ken, Japan** — 3-2884-8 Higashisayanagaoka, Tokorozawa-shi, Saitama-Ken, Japan 359; **Selangor, Malaysia** — No. 18 Jalan 6/6, Petaling Jaya / 564957.

AUSTRALASIA

Adelaide, Australia — 13-A Frome St. / (08)223-2084; **Auckland, New Zealand** — Hwy. 18, Riverhead (next to Huapai Golfcourse) (mail: c/o R.D. 2, Kumeu) / 412-8075; **Brisbane, Australia** — 56 Bellevue Terrace, St. Lucia 4066, Queensland; **Christchurch, New Zealand** — 30 Latimer Sq.; **Jakarta, Indonesia** — Jalan Rawamangun Muka Timur 80 / 4835-19; **Lautoka, Fiji** — 5 Tavewa Ave. (mail: c/o P.O. Box 125) / 61-633, ext. 48; **Melbourne, Australia** — 197 Danks St., Albert Park, Melbourne, Victoria 3206 (mail: c/o P.O. Box 125) / 699-5122; **Perth, Australia** — P.O. Box 299, Subiaco, 6008, Perth, Western Australia; **Sydney, Australia** — 112 Darlinghurst Rd., King's Cross, N.S.W. (mail: c/o P.O. Box 159) / (02)357-5162.

FARMS: Auckland, New Zealand (New Varshana) — contact ISKCON Auckland; **Colo, Australia (Bhaktivedanta Ashram)** — Upper Colo Rd., N.S.W. (mail: c/o P.O. Box 493, St. Mary's, 2760, N.S.W.) / 045-75-5284; **Murwillumbah, Australia (New Govardhana)** — 'Eungella,' Tyalgum Rd. via Murwillumbah, N.S.W. 2484 (mail: c/o P.O. Box 687) / 066-72-1903.

RESTAURANTS: Adelaide — Govinda's, 13 Frome Street; **Melbourne** — Gopal's, 237 Flinders Lane / 63 1578; **Melbourne** — Gopal's, 251 Malvern Road, South Yarrow; **Sydney** — Mukunda's, 233 Victoria Street, Darlinghurst / 357 5162.

EUROPE

Amsterdam, Holland — Keizersgracht 94 / 020-249 410; **Antwerp, Belgium** — 25 Katelijnevest / 031-320987; **Athens, Greece** — 133 Solonos; **Catania, Sicily** — Via Empedocle 84, 95100 / 095-522-252; **Copenhagen, Denmark** — Korfuvej 9, 2300 Copenhagen S / 972337; **Dublin, Ireland** — 2 Belvedere Place, Dublin 1 / 743-767; **Duedingen, Switzerland** — Im Stillen Tal, CH 3186 Duedingen (FR) / (037) 43.26.97; **Gallarate, Italy** — Via A. Volta 19, Gallarate 20131 (VA) / 0331-783-268; **Göthenburg, Sweden** — Karl Gustavsgatan 19, 41125 Göthenburg / 031-110955; **Heidelberg, W. Germany** — Vrindavana, Plöck 54; **London, England (city)** — 10 Soho St., London W1 / 01-437-3662; **London, England (country)** — Bhaktivedanta Manor, Letchmore Heath, Watford, Hertfordshire WD2 8EP / Radlett 7244; **Madrid, Spain** — Calle Arturo Sorio No. 209; **Munich, W. Germany** — Govinda's Club, Kaulbachstrasse 1, 8000 Munchen / 089-280807; **Paris, France** — 20 rue Vieille du Temple, Paris 75004 / 500-63-58; **Rome, Italy** — Salita del Poggio Laurentino 7, Rome 00144 / (06)593-075; **Septon, Belgium** — Chateau de Petit Somme, Septon 5482 / 086-322480; **Stockholm, Sweden** — Korsnas Gård, 140 32 Grödinge / 0753-29151; **Vienna, Austria** — Govinda Kulturzentrum, Lerchenfelderstrasse 17, A-1070 Wien / (0222) 96 10 633; **West Berlin, W. Germany** — Potsdamerstrasse 70, 1 Berlin W. 30 / 030-262-1447; **Worcester, England** — Chaitanya College at Croome Court, Severn Stoke, Worcester WR8 9DW / 090 567-214; **Zürich, Switzerland** — Bergstrasse 54, 8032 Zürich / (01)693388.

FARMS: Bavarian Forest (Bayrische-Wald), W. Germany (Nava-Jīyada-Nrsimha-Kṣetra) — (contact ISKCON Munich); **Brihuega, Spain (New Vraja Mandala)** — (Santa Clara) Brihuega, Guadalajara / (11) 280018; **Florence, Italy (Villa Vrndāvana)** — Via Comunale degli Scopeti, No. 108, St. Andrea in Percussina, San Casciano Val di Pesa 56030 (Firenze) / 055-820054; **London, England** — (contact Bhaktivedanta Manor); **Valencay, France (New Mayapur)** — Lucay-Le-Male, 36 600 / (54) 40-23-26.

RESTAURANTS: London — Healthy, Wealthy, and Wise, 9-10 Soho Street / 01-437-1835; **Stockholm** — Govinda's, Grevgatan 18, 114 53 Stockholm / 08-623411; **Vienna** — Govinda (at ISKCON Vienna); **Zürich** — Govinda, Brandschenkestrasse 12, 8002 Zürich / (01)2029282.

LATIN AMERICA

BRAZIL: Curitiba, Paraná — Rua Profa, Maria Assumpaco 77, Vila Hauer, 80.000 / 276-6274; **Pindamonhangaba, SP** — Rua Dom Joao Bosco 848, Santana; **Pôrto Alegre, RS** — Rua Giordano Bruno 318, 90.000; **Recife, Pernambuco** — Ave. 17 de Agosto 257, Parnamirim 50.000; **Rio de Janeiro, RJ** — Estrada dos Tres Rios 654, Jacarepagua, 22.700; **Salvador Bahia** — Rua Alvaro Adorno 17, Brotas, 40.000 / (071)240-1072; **São Paulo, SP** — Rua Pandia Calogeras 54, 01525 / (011)270-3442.

FARM: Pindamonhangaba, São Paulo (New Gokula) — Ribeirao Grande (mail: C.P. 108, 12.400 Pindamonhangaba) / 2797836.

OTHER COUNTRIES: Bogotá, Colombia — Carrera 3A No. 54-A-72 / 255-9842; **Cuzco, Peru** — Avenida Pardo No. 1036 / 2277; **Georgetown, Guyana** — 24 Uitvlugt Front, West Coast Demerara; **Guadalajara, Mexico** — Avenida las Americas No. 225, Sector Hidalgo / 163455; **Guatemala City, Guatemala** — Sexta Avenida 1-89, Zona 1 / 24618; **La Paz, Bolivia** — Calle Chacaltaya No. 587 / 32-85-67; **Lima, Peru** — Jiron Junin 415 / 47-18-10; **Medellin, Colombia** — Carrera 32, No. 54-42; **Mexico City, Mexico** — Gob. Tiburcio Montiel 45, San Miguel Chapultepec, Mexico D.F. 18 / (905)271-0132; **Monterrey, Mexico** — General Albino Espinoza, 345 Pte., Zona Centro, Monterrey, N.L. / 42 67 66; **Panama City, Panama** — 43-58 Via España Altos, Al Lado del Cine, Bella Vista; **Puebla, Mexico** — Sierra Madre 9010, Colonia Maravillas, Pueblo Quito, Ecuador — Apdo. 2384, Calle Yasuni No. 404; **St. Augustine, Trinidad and Tobago** — Gordon St. at Santa Margarita Circular Rd. / 662-4605; **San José, Costa Rica** — 400 mtrs. Sur Centro Médico de Guadalupe (casa blanca esquinera) Colonia Chapultepec, Guadalupe; **San Salvador, El Salvador** — 67 Avenida Sur No. 115, Colonia Escalo; **Santiago, Chile** — Eyzaguirre 2404, Casilla 44, Puente Alto / 283; **Santo Domingo, Dominican Republic** — Calle Cayatano Rodriguez No. 254 / (809)688-7242; **Valparaiso, Chile** — Colon 2706 / 7099; **Vera Cruz, Mexico** — Calle 3 Carabelas No. 784, Fraccionmiento Reforma, Vera Cruz.

NORTH AMERICA

CANADA: Edmonton, Alberta — 10132 142nd St., T5N 2N7 / (403)452-5855; **Montreal, Quebec** — 1626 Pie IX Boulevard, H1V 2C5 / (514) 527-1101; **Ottawa, Ontario** — 212 Somerset St. E., K1N 6V4 / (613)233-3460; **Toronto, Ontario** — 243 Avenue Rd. M5R 2J6 / (416)922-5415; **Vancouver, B.C.** — 5580 S.E. Marine Dr., Burnaby V5J 3G8 / (604)430-4437; **Victoria, B.C.** — 4056 Rainbow St., V8X 2A9 / (604)479-0649.

FARM: Hemingford, Quebec (New Nandagram) — 315 Backbrush Rd., RR. No. 2, J0L 1H0 / (514)247-3429.

RESTAURANTS: Toronto — Govinda's, 1280 Bay St. / (416)968-1313; **Vancouver** — Govinda's, 1221 Thurlow / (604)682-8154.

U.S.A.: Atlanta, Georgia — 1287 Ponce de Leon Ave. NE 30306 / (404)378-9182; **Baltimore, Maryland** — 200 Bloomsbury Ave, Catonsville 21228 / (301)788-3883; **Berkeley, California** — 2334 Stuart St. 94705 / (415) 843-7874; **Boston, Massachusetts** — 72 Commonwealth Ave. 02116 / (617)536-1695; **Chicago, Illinois** — 1716 West Lunt Ave. 60626 / (312)973-0900; **Cleveland, Ohio** — 15720 Euclid Ave., E. Cleveland 44112 / (216)851-9367; **Columbus, Ohio** — 99 East 13th Ave. 43201 / (614) 299-5084; **Dallas, Texas** — 5430 Gurley Ave. 75223 / (214)827-6330; **Denver, Colorado** — 1400 Cherry St. 80220 / (303)333-5461; **Detroit, Michigan** — 383 Lenox Ave. 48215 / (313)824-6000; **E. Lansing, Michigan** — 319 Grove St. 48823 / (517)351-6603; **Gainesville, Florida** — Rt. 2, Box 24, Alachua, 32615 / (904)462-1143; **Hartford, Connecticut** — 1683 Main St., East Hartford 06108 / (203)528-1600; **Honolulu, Hawaii** — 51 Coelho Way 96817 / (808)595-3947; **Houston, Texas** — 1111 Rosalie St. 77004 / (713)526-9860; **Laguna Beach, California** — 644 S. Coast Hwy. 92651 / (714)497-3638; **Las Vegas, Nevada** — 5805 Alta Dr. 87066 / (702)870-6638; **Long Island, New York** — 197 S. Ocean Ave., Freeport 11520 / (516)378-6184; **Los Angeles, California** — 3764 Watseka Ave. 90034 / (213)558-9016; **Miami Beach, Florida** — 2445 Collins Ave. 33140 / (305)531-0331; **Newark, Delaware** — 168 Elkton Rd. 19711 / (302)453-8510; **New Orleans, Louisiana** — 2936 Esplanade Ave. 70119 / (504)488-7433; **New York, New York** — 340 W. 55th St. 10019 / (212)765-8610; **Philadelphia, Pennsylvania** — 41-51 West Allens Lane, 19119 / (215)247-4600; **Pittsburgh, Pennsylvania** — 1112 N. Negley Ave. 15206 / (412)362-0212; **Portland, Oregon** — 2805 S.E. Hawthorne St. 97214 / (503)231-5792; **St. Louis, Missouri** — 3926 Lindell Blvd. 63108 / (314)535-8085; **San Diego, California** — 1030 Grand Ave., Pacific Beach 92109 / (714)483-2500; **San Francisco, California** — 1403 Willard St., 94117 / (415)664-7724; **San Juan, Puerto Rico** — 1015 Ponce de Leon St., Rio Piedras, 00925 / (809)765-4745; **Seattle, Washington** — 400 18th Ave. East 98112 / (206)322-3636; **State College, Pennsylvania** — 103 E. Hamilton Ave. 16801 / (814)234-1867; **Washington, D.C.** — 10310 Oaklyn Rd., Potomac, Maryland 20854 / (301)299-2100.

FARMS: Carriere, Mississippi (New Tālavan) — Rt. No. 2, Box 449, 39426 / (601)798-6705; **Gainesville, Florida** — contact ISKCON Gainesville; **Gurabo, Puerto Rico (New Gandhamadana)** — Box 215, B, Route 181, Santar ia 00658; **Hopland, California (New Vraja-maṇḍala Dhāma)** — Route 175, Box 469, 95449 / (707)744-1100; **Hotchkiss, Colorado (New Barshana)** — P.O. Box 112, 81419 / (303)527-4584; **Lynchburg, Tennessee (Murāri-sevaka)** — Rt. No. 1, Box 146-A, (Mulberry) 37359 / (615)759-7058; **Moundsville, West Virginia (New Vrindaban)** — R.D. No. 1, Box 319, Hare Krishna Ridge 26041 / (304)845-2790; **Port Royal, Pennsylvania (Gita-nāgari)** — R.D. No. 1, 17082 / (717)-527-2493.

RESTAURANTS: Columbus, Ohio — Simply Wonderful, 2044 High Street 43201 / (614)299-6132; **Los Angeles** — Govinda's, 9634 Venice Blvd., Culver City 90230 / (213)836-1269; **New York, New York** — (at ISKCON New York); **St. Louis, Missouri** — (at ISKCON St. Louis) / (341)535-8161; **San Juan, Puerto Rico** — Govinda's (at ISKCON San Juan); **Washington, D.C.** — Govinda's, 515 8th St. S.E. 20003 / (202)543-9600.